Successful
Science and Engineering Teaching
in Colleges and Universities

Successful
Science and Engineering Teaching
in Colleges and Universities

Calvin S. Kalman
Concordia University

ANKER PUBLISHING COMPANY, INC.
Bolton, Massachusetts

Successful Science and Engineering Teaching
in Colleges and Universities

ISBN 978-1-933371-16-0

Composition by Lyn Rodger, Deerfoot Studios
Cover design by Dutton & Sherman Design

Anker Publishing Company, Inc.
563 Main Street
P.O. Box 249
Bolton, MA 01740-0249 USA

www.ankerpub.com

Library of Congress Cataloging-in-Publication Data

Kalman, C. S. (Calvin S.)
 Successful science and engineering teaching in colleges and universities / Calvin S. Kalman.
    p. cm.
 Includes bibliographical references and index.
 ISBN-13: 978-1-933371-16-0
 1. Science—Study and teaching (Higher) 2. Engineering—Study and teaching (Higher) 3. Effective teaching. I. Title.

Q181.K35 2007
507.1'1—dc22
                        2006032608

This volume is dedicated to my wife Judy (February 23, 1946–June 29, 2006), our children Ben and Sam, and our grandson Josh. This work would never have come to fruition if it were not for my wife's inspiration and ideas, as well as her unflagging support and encouragement. She was a truly great teacher and a model for my own teaching.

Table of Contents

About the Author

Calvin S. Kalman is a tenured full professor in the Department of Physics, a fellow of the Science College, and a member of the Centre for the Study of Learning and Performance at Concordia University. He is also an adjunct professor in the Department of Educational and Counselling Psychology at McGill University. He has held many positions at Concordia, including chair of the physics department. He has served as chair of the international series of conferences on hyperons, charm and beauty hadrons (Montreal 1997, Genoa 1998, Valencia 2000, Vancouver 2002, Chicago 2004, Lancaster UK 2006). He also served as editor-in-chief for the proceedings of these conferences. In addition, he has cochaired and coedited the 26th annual Montreal-Rochester-Syracuse-Toronto (MRST) conference on high energy physics and coauthored the book *Preons: Models of Leptons, Quarks and Gauge Bosons as Composite Particles* (1992, World Scientific). He held the positions of science editor and senior executive editor of *Academic Exchange Quarterly.*

The author of 73 published papers related to high energy physics and 34 papers on science educational research, he has also been invited to give papers and workshops on educational research. He presented the keynote address at the annual spring teaching forum, Teaching the Future: Innovation in the College Classroom, at Yale University and at the annual meeting of the physics and engineering physics division of the American Society for Electrical Engineers.

Professor Kalman has served as commissioner for elementary schools and also as commissioner for high schools of the Protestant School Board of Greater Montreal. He also served on the council of the Canadian Association of Physicists. He was awarded the Canadian Association of Physicists Medal for Excellence in Teaching, the Concordia University Council on Student Life Teaching Award, and a Teaching and Creativity Award from the Society for Teaching and Learning in Higher Education.

Acknowledgments

My wife, Judy Kalman, who has had many successes in teaching writing at Concordia University and Dawson College, has inspired many of my efforts to bring writing into the science classroom. She convinced me to set aside my initial skepticism about writing methods such as journaling and attend an intensive two-day workshop at the University of Vermont that impressed me enough to try some new techniques such as the course dossier method. She and Marjorie McKinnon were instrumental in convincing me to use collaborative groups in my teaching. At the time, Marjorie was associate director of the Concordia University Centre for Faculty Development. My first efforts in innovative teaching based on computer-assisted instruction would never have come to fruition without the help of Ron Smith and David Kaufman. Craig Nelson, whom I have never met, inspired my idea to follow conceptual conflict collaborative group exercises with a writing activity. Without the support of and many discussions with Mark Aulls, I would not have learned how reflective writing works. This book owes much to Carolyn Dumore, managing editor at Anker Publishing Company. She carefully went over every word of the book and provided many helpful suggestions for revisions. I would like to thank Teresa Larkin for sharing the guidelines and Call for Papers that she used in spring 2005 along with recent brochures to illustrate my discussion of her End-of-Semester Conference. Some parts of this book have appeared in articles I wrote for *American Journal of Physics, Science and Education,* and *Academic Exchange Quarterly.* I wish to thank Thomson Learning and Heinemann for granting me permission to reproduce and/or paraphrase some material in this book.

Author Note

This book is intentionally informal. In writing it, I viewed it as a discussion of our mutual interest in helping students learn. I hope that you will continue the conversation by letting me know what works for you and how you may have changed this material in ways that work better in your courses.

Calvin S. Kalman
Kalman@vax2.concordia.ca

1

Introduction

I have always been interested in ways of improving the teaching of science. In my teaching assistant days, I was given the opportunity to teach a class of 300 students for a month instead of just my recitation section. I used the opportunity to try a unique presentation of the material. In my efforts to improve my teaching and later to research teaching science at the college and university level, I have turned not only to research in physics education, but also to developments in postsecondary education in other areas of science and in engineering. My first paper in educational research was coauthored by an engineer and a mathematician (Kalman, Kaufman, & Smith, 1974). My work on using writing to help students learn was particularly influenced by educational research on writing-to-learn by mathematicians, and some of my efforts have been influenced by the seminal work of biology professor Craig Nelson. One of my most enthusiastic supporters at Concordia University is a faculty member who invited me to address the engineering faculty on ways that writing could help engineering students to understand the course content.

Before beginning to use this book, I would like you to explore your ideas about teaching. I have two reasons for asking you to do this:

1) To introduce you to a tool for exploring concepts called *reflective writing*. I ask all students in every course from the introductory level to the graduate level to use this tool to explore concepts in their textbook before they discuss the concepts in class. It would be helpful if you were acquainted with this tool before I discuss it later in this book.

2) In introductory courses, one problem is changing students' epistemologies from their uninstructed viewpoints to the epistemology of their textbook. One of the most successful approaches is for them to compare various sets of concepts and to discover that they are in conflict. Indeed, Feyerabend (1993) has pointed out that evaluation of a theoretical framework doesn't occur until there is an alternative (principle of counter induction). I would like you to clearly enunciate your philosophy of teaching and to compare it with my philosophy as you explore this book. I hope that this will aid you in using this book and in examining the utility of Feyerabend's principle of counter induction.

I will now briefly introduce how to use reflective writing to explore your ideas about teaching. There is a more extended examination of reflective writing in Chapter 2. Reflective writing is based on freewriting, popularized by Elbow (1998). In reflective writing, you freewrite to explore a concept or a piece of writing such as a section of a textbook. Countryman (1992) defines freewriting as writing rapidly for a short, fixed period. Start writing and keep writing. Write about what the reading means. Have a conversation with yourself in your writing. One student said, "It's a little bit like thinking out loud and then putting it on paper. . . . It's quite surprising to see how much more it's helpful once it's put down on paper."

Now, take out a sheet of paper and use reflective writing to explore your ideas about teaching. When you have finished the freewriting, reread it and underline the main points so that you can compare your ideas with those presented in this book.

Teacher-Centered Learning

In teacher-centered learning, the professor lectures, makes presentations, and provides opportunities for students to answer questions (See Figure 1.1). Students do assignments as required. I should make clear at the outset that I am not opposed to lecturing—I lecture in all but one of my courses. But I lecture in small doses punctuated by student-centered activities. Teacher-centered learning as I refer to it is essentially lecturing with demonstrations managed by the instructor and short question-and-answer periods also managed by the instructor. When does learning take place? Obviously, some learning takes place when students do the assignments, but is this the kind of learning that the instructor desires? Paul Hewitt (1995), author of the best-selling book *Conceptual Physics,* writes, "The professor and the students view solving of problems in a very different way. The professor classifies the problems in terms of concepts, while the students classify them by situations" (p. 85). Some students can dismiss the conceptual basis of the problems because their epistemology is formula driven and they accept calculated answers as a goal in itself. Such students are so resistant that they may claim that professors are not doing the job if they teach concepts. They insist that professors spend as much time as possible working problems in class.

> *One goal of an introductory science course is to change the student's epistemology from a view that study in science is a matter of solving problems using techniques classified according to problem type, to a view that a science subject consists of a web of interconnected concepts.*

FIGURE 1.1
Teacher-Centered Learning

Course content

↓

Professor lectures, takes responsibility for learning

↓

Students try to understand the concepts. When?
That night? Next week? Just before the exam?

Problem-solving skills require knowledge of concepts. Until midway through high school, students can be successful at courses by memorizing templates for every situation encountered on an examination. That is, they apply different templates to different knowledge subsets. Students lack the ability to apply principles garnered from a problem to an apparently different problem. Examine the following story from Gick and Holyoak (1980, 1983) and Duncker's (1945) "radiation problem" that follows it.

> A small country was ruled from a strong fortress by a dictator. The fortress was situated in the middle of the country, surrounded by farms and villages. Many roads led to the fortress through the countryside. A rebel general vowed to capture the fortress. The general knew that an attack by his entire army would capture the fortress. He gathered his army at the head of one of the roads, ready to launch a full-scale direct attack. However, the general then learned that the dictator had planted mines on each of the roads. The mines were set so that small bodies of men could pass over them safely, since the dictator needed to move his troops and workers to and from the fortress. However, any large force would detonate the mines. Not only would this blow up the road, but it would also destroy many neighboring villages. It therefore seemed impossible to capture the fortress. However, the general devised a simple plan. He divided his army into small groups and dispatched each group to the head of a different road. When all was ready, he gave the signal and each group marched down a different road. Each group continued down its road to the fortress so that the entire army arrived together at the fortress at the same time. In this way, the general captured the fortress and overthrew the dictator. (qtd. in Vander-Stoep & Seifert, 1994, p. 29)

> Suppose you are a doctor faced with a patient who has a malignant tumor in his stomach. It is impossible to operate on the patient, but unless the tumor is destroyed, the patient will die. There is a kind of ray that can be used to destroy the tumor. If the rays reach the tumor all at once at a sufficiently high intensity, the tumor will be destroyed. Unfortunately, at this intensity, the healthy tissue that the rays pass through on the way to the tumor will also be destroyed. At lower intensities, the rays are harmless to healthy tissue, but they will not affect the tumor either. What type of procedure might be used to destroy the tumor with the rays, and at the same time, avoid destroying the healthy tissue? (qtd. in VanderStoep & Seifert, 1994, p. 30)

Would your students recognize that the story and the radiation problem are the same problem? Students see problems worked out in class. When they begin to do their assignments, they use these problems and the solved problems in the book to find ones that are like their homework problems. They complain that they understand how to do the problems done in class and those found in the book, but they do not know how to do some of their assigned problems. Yet the problems that they cannot do may be as similar to problems done in class and the solved problems in the textbook as the story by Gick and Holyoak is to Dunker's radiation problem. If students understand the underlying concepts, they know how to solve these problems. However, the learning that occurs during a teacher-centered course is often only learning about solving specific problems. When do students try to understand the concepts? The night of the lecture? A week later? A week before the exam? Perhaps the day before the exam? What expertise can students call on to help them when they try to understand concepts?

> *Students should sort out how well they understand the concepts before the class starts, then use the class as an opportunity to try and understand the concepts while the professor is available as a source of expertise.*

FIGURE 1.2

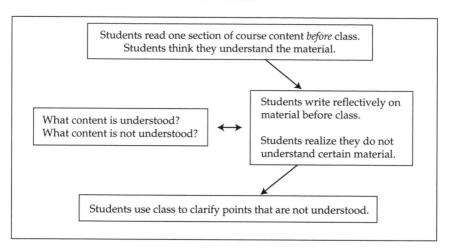

Reflective writing is not writing in the traditional sense, but rather a tool that allows students to engage metacognitively with the material in the textbook. *Metacognitive*—thinking about your thinking—is a self-dialogue about what you understand. Compare it with what happens when we talk to someone about a problem. The person we talk to does not really contribute to the solution. As we outline the problem, we start to solve the problem, and indeed solve it without any help.

Road Map of the Book

Student-centered learning as presented in this book is comprised of a number of elements. These include getting students to write reflectively on the material in the textbook before they come to class. Students may also be asked to engage in group work both in and out of class and to engage in various writing activities. One professor who began using a student-centered approach commented that a great weight had been lifted off his shoulders. He no longer felt that he was responsible for student learning. He was sharing the responsibility with the students.

> If we want to adopt the view that we want to teach
> as many as possible of our students then we must

> adopt a mix of approaches and be prepared that some of them will not work for some students. (Redish, 2003, p. 38)

In addition to the objectives already discussed, we should recognize that students' learning styles are not homogeneous. Why do students disagree about their experiences with the same professor? Leaving aside gifted teachers, opinions about professors vary markedly from student to student. One major reason is that students learn differently. Some students have a great deal of difficulty learning if they do not have aural stimulation. At home, they may learn best if they have loud music blaring while they study. Others may learn by recopying their notes. Some need to work individually. Others find talking to other students useful. A variety of different activities is helpful.

As professors, we tend to emulate a favorite teacher. This teacher is likely to have taught us in ways that correspond to our own learning style. We need to consciously adopt many approaches to learning to facilitate learning by as many students in the class as possible, not just use approaches that work for us.

Writing-to-Learn

After Chapter 2 on reflective writing, Chapters 3 and 7 will consider other uses of writing-to-learn in science and engineering. Writing-to-learn helps students learn how to learn and to apply what they learn, rather than memorize what an expert has established. In Chapter 3, the course dossier method will be presented. I have used this method in courses where students use writing to examine the course as a whole. I use this method in the most advanced course in our undergraduate curriculum, Advanced Classical Electrodynamics. In general education courses, I use the course dossier method in place of an examination.

Two Goals for Any Science Course

1) Get students to sort out how much they understand about concepts before the class starts and use the class as an opportunity

to try and understand the concepts while the professor is available as a source of expertise.

2) Get students to critically examine their ideas about the material presented in the course and in general to improve their critical thinking skills.

Questions by Students

Since I want my students to come to class with some knowledge of the material that I will discuss in class, I use reflective writing in all my courses, from introductory through the Ph.D. level. Students are informed that some of the material and problems found in the text in their readings will *not* be covered in class, but the exam will be based on everything found in these readings. I assume that if students are successful in passing the prerequisites for the course, they are capable of reading and understanding the simpler concepts. Since I don't take class time to cover these concepts, I have more time to do problems in class and to use other activities in class such as discussions (in pairs, small groups, or whole class). If, contrary to my expectations, a student has a problem with some concept in the reading that I do not discuss in class, I would expect the student to ask about it in class.

> *It is not good practice to ask if there are any questions and after a short time move on. This indicates you believe that almost the entire class understands what you are talking about, when frequently many students are puzzled.*

Try to make your class a safe environment where students feel comfortable asking questions. I consider that any question that a student asks is a reasonable question. I tell students that I almost never get a stupid question. When a student is really off topic, I pronounce the question to be interesting, but one that I would like to discuss with the student in my office. I try and give encouraging remarks about all questions: "You are really helping us with that question." "I am glad you asked that. I am sure that many people in the class were wondering about that point." "All of you have helped us understand this topic. She (pointing) got us started, and he (pointing) moved us along, and then she (pointing) provided us with a fuller understanding." Remarks like these get students to feel that the class is a safe environment. Once that atmosphere is established, you receive many questions, even in large classes.

> *Students will ask questions if they feel that the class is a*
> *safe, secure environment.*

I never embarrass students with my responses. I also don't ask any particular student to answer a question. If the same handful of students answer all the time, I may suggest that I need some other students to answer questions. Many teachers ask the class questions and after a short silence, answer the question themselves. I never answer questions that I pose to the class. Students are often reluctant to answer a question, but if you wait, it is likely that a student will fill the silence by answering. I usually take an insulated mug with coffee or tea in it, which is a great prop. Ask a question. No answer. Take the mug. Sip slowly and relax. Once students start answering, gradually move the responses to encourage more responses. "That's a good response but not quite right." "Thanks for that one. That's not it, but you have started our search." If the class is really having trouble, I might give some hints. Rarely, the class really can't answer. I then ask them to work on it and come back with the answer next class.

> *Never answer a question yourself that you ask the class.*
> *Many professors don't wait long enough.*

What Students Get Out of Class

Many years ago I attended a workshop given by Graham Gibbs, a noted expert on study skills. He related the following experience: He had been asked by a well-known historian to help his class with note taking. Consequently, he attended a class to observe, and was to speak about note taking during the last five minutes of class. The professor was speaking about voyages to North America and was such an engaging speaker that Gibbs forgot why he was at the class. He seemed even to smell the salt water carried by the wind. With a start, he remembered why he was there and looked around the class. Surprisingly, at even the most interesting parts, students were staring out the window! This revelation led him to tear up his notes. At the end of the class, he handed the professor a transparency. "Write down the three most important points that you wanted students to take away from this class," he instructed the professor. Then he asked the students to write down the three most important points that they had derived from the class. How many of the students wrote down the points that the professor asked them to carry away from the class?

After the professor displayed the transparency, the expert asked how many students had noted all the points that the professor had written on the transparency. Not a single student had. How many students had written down one point? Again, not a single student had. How many students had written down one of the three points that the professor wanted them to take away from the class? A few students near the front timidly raised their hands. Why had this happened? Students have their own views of our courses. Indeed, they often mishear what we say in class and misread what is written in the textbook. We see what we *expect* to see and we read what we *expect* to read. A similar situation relates to how fights sometimes break out between friends. Two friends become angry at each other for days, weeks, perhaps even months, until one of them discovers through the efforts of mutual acquaintances that the friend did not say what he or she thought the friend had said. The friend's utterances had been misheard!

> At times, we need special activities to make our most important points clear to students.

In-Class and Out-of-Class Activities

In Chapter 4, the misconceptions that students carry with them into their courses are examined. In subsequent chapters, activities that help students to examine their conceptual framework so that they will not mishear their instructor or misread their textbook are presented. Research shows that most students have loosely organized course concepts in contrast to the web of interconnections perceived by their instructors (Hammer, 1989, 1994). Elby (2001) has said that "students' epistemological beliefs—their views about the nature of knowledge and learning—affect their mindset, metacognitive practices, and study habits in a physics course" (p. S64). Developing a scientific/engineering mindset thus may not simply be a conceptual change from personal scientific/engineering concepts to scientifically accepted concepts. It may also be a change in attitude from a view that study in science and engineering is a matter of solving problems using techniques that are classified according to problem type, to a view that a science/engineering subject consists of a web of interconnected concepts. Background about the process of epistemological change is included in the discussion on critical thinking in Chapter 4. Chapters 5 and 6 examine activities, particularly small-group activities, that can be used to promote epistemological change. Applications of small-group activities to develop epistemological change are found in Chapter 7.

Solving Problems

Various methods for helping students solve problems are found in Chapters 8 and 9. Chapter 8 considers the general difficulty of helping students to solve problems and Chapter 9 presents two methods effective in getting them to overcome their anxieties and become expert problem solvers. The methods are based on the two main themes of the book: reflective writing and collaborative groups.

Computer Aids

Using computers to give tutorial lessons is one of two subjects discussed in Chapter 10. A modification of Noah Sherman's (1971) templates is included that can easily be used to construct your own tutorial programs. Also included is a tutorial program that I have used with some success in my classroom. How to manage your laboratories using the computer is also presented.

Summary

- *We need to consciously adopt many approaches to learning to facilitate learning by as many students in the class as possible including, for example, not only approaches that work for us. We may use more than one activity to reach the same pedagogical objective.*

- *Do you agree with the discussion about teacher-centered and student-centered classrooms? Nothing is ever really black and white. Most likely you use a mixture of both forms of teaching. This would be a good time to evaluate your teaching.*

- *Collaborative group activities discussed in Chapters 5, 6, and 7 can be used in your classroom—even if it is a large class of more than 100 students—for discussions to take place in your classroom.*

- *Would you like your students to come to grips with the material in the textbook before you discuss it in class? The reflective writing techniques found in Chapter 2 provide a way to make this happen. Writing can be used in many other ways to help students understand concepts, as discussed in Chapters 3 and 7.*

- *Are students intellectually prepared for your course? This subject is developed in Chapter 4, along with how to promote critical thinking in your course.*

- *Do your students have difficulty solving problems? The general difficulty of helping students to solve problems and two methods effective in getting them to overcome their anxieties and become expert problem solvers are presented in Chapter 9.*

- *Do your students need extensive remedial attention that cannot be provided in a recitation section? The answer might be a computer-assisted tutorial program as described in Chapter 10. Computers can help students get more out of lab work by using the computer-managed system described in Chapter 10. It can also save money on your lab budget.*

2

Reflective Writing

When students arrive in class, they should be prepared to discuss the material that will be presented. Students should not read the assigned material just before class, but actually engage with it, trying to sort out what they understand and what they do not understand. This is what happens when students examine material in their textbook using reflective writing—gathering thoughts on a chosen topic, then rethinking to develop knowledge. Reflective writing is not writing in the traditional sense, but rather a process that allows students to engage *metacognitively* with some given material. Metacognition means thinking about your thinking. The writing is used by students to construct a self-dialogue about what they understand. In this chapter, I describe reflective writing, how it works, and how students use it to metacognitively examine material in the textbook before coming to class. After using reflective writing for several weeks, most students really like it. Consequently, I use it in every course from the introductory level through the highest-level graduate course. Additionally, it can be used in class, in a manner that helps to generate discussion about difficult concepts, which will be discussed in the next chapter.

There are other methods to get students to read assigned material before classes; for example, having students take quizzes on the chapter in class or having students summarize the material in the chapter and hand in the summary each week. However, neither of these methods helps students to metacognitively engage with the material before attending class. Students report that engaging with the material using reflective writing increases their reading comprehension and they are more conscious of what they do or do not understand during writing.

> Reflective writing has been a very beneficial experience for me. . . . Through reflective writing I was given the opportunity to write on a more regular basis and assess my writing skills continually. To anyone considering reflective writing, I suggest an open mind and discipline. In the end, you discover areas where you need improving. I strongly feel that due to reflective writing my reading comprehension level has increased and I have become a more conscious writer. I have therefore noticed a significant grade increase.
>
> —*Note sent by a student to help future students*

Reflective writing involves reading a section of a textbook, then using a form of writing called freewriting as a tool to self-dialogue about the concepts found in the section. First, we will examine what comprises freewriting and how to do it, then we will consider how the self-dialogue works. This is followed by a discussion of how students perform the reflective writing activity, including the instructions given to the students, and student reactions to the activity.

Freewriting

Freewriting can be used when students read assignments, discuss the content, and then engage in freewriting to help internalize the concepts and conceptual relationships. Freewriting, popularized by Elbow (1998), falls within Britton's notion of expressive writing (Britton, Burgess, Martin, McLeod, & Rosen, 1975). Britton uses the term *expressive writing* to refer to writing to oneself, as in diaries, journals, and first-draft papers, or to writing to trusted people who are very close to the writer, as in personal letters. Since it is not intended for external audiences, it has few constraints of form and style. Expressive writing often looks like speech written down. Usually it is characterized by first-person pronouns, informal style, and colloquial diction. Fulwiler (1987) comments, "Some writing activities promote independent thought more than others do. Expressive or self-sponsored writing, for example, seems to advance thought further than rote copying" (p. 21).

Countryman (1992) defines freewriting as writing rapidly for a short, fixed period of time. During freewriting, you should not stop writing except to move your pen from one word to the other. If at any time you feel that you can't go on—your mind is a blank— write a "nonsense" word over and over, for example, the last word that you wrote, wrote, wrote, wrote . . . until you start writing again. The writing produced lacks many of the grammatical features found in essay writing. Naturally, if you are not used to freewriting, you feel that it is unsatisfactory. It takes time to get used to writing without stopping to edit your work. Many examples of freewriting are found in Fulwiler (1987), including a section on writing in college physics by Verner Jensen. Jensen proposes that "understanding can be enhanced through a freewriting experience" and that "physics students can use the writing process to clarify their thinking and understandings about physical phenomena through their written articulation of relationships. Learning physics requires many different mind processes including abstract thinking. Writing can assist the student with this process" (p. 330).

In the following piece on the kinetic theory of molecules, a student was asked to write to a roommate who is assumed to know little about science. The student is to freewrite about the kinetic theory of gases.

> The kinetic theory of molecules is a really neat topic
> . . . and I'm sure you'd like to hear about it! In this
> theory we see how particles in a box relate to each
> other. The particles in a box are in constant motion,
> bouncing off each other and bouncing off the walls
> of the box. Some move up and down, some left and

right, and some forward and backward. One aspect of the theory is that the length of the box sides will affect the time between collisions. Also, the faster the molecules move, the less time there will be between collisions. Kinetic energy, the energy produced as a result of motion, is the result of one-half the mass of the particle times the velocity squared of the particle.

Let's look at the velocity of one particle. It will depend on two factors. First, the larger the box, the faster the particle will move after bouncing around. Second, the smaller the molecule, the faster it will be able to move. An analogy would be a warm room. The larger the room and the heavier the gas, will affect the rate at which the particles hit you—make you warm! As the molecules move faster they travel greater distances especially if their mass is small. (Jensen, 1987, p. 332)

In this piece, we see the characteristic informal nature of freewriting. The first paragraph wanders as the student explores the topic. Note that the writing in the second paragraph is much more formal and the ideas used by the student to write the paragraph came out of the informal freewriting found in the first paragraph. As one freewrites, one's thoughts may drift in many directions. To be effective, the freewrite must be directed to a specific topic—in this example, the kinetic theory of gases.

The Bereiter and Scardamalia Model

Let's consider the freewriting piece on the kinetic theory of gases in the context of the work of Bereiter and Scardamalia (1987) to illustrate why it is not fruitful to have a student read a section of the textbook and then summarize what was read. Summarizing a piece of writing falls within what Bereiter and Scardamalia refer to as the *knowledge telling model.* Such writing is essentially linear and does not get students to reflect on their writing. The second paragraph of our freewriting sample is a more developed mode of writing, which Bereiter and Scardamalia refer to as the *knowledge transforming model*. Students can be directed to use freewriting to reflect on the concepts found in the assigned section and sort out their understanding of the concepts to learn how much they understand or do not understand. They will then be prepared to use their time in the classroom to gain understanding of the material through effective listening and questioning.

The Knowledge Telling Model

The following description of the knowledge telling model is based on the work of Bereiter and Scardamalia (1987). In this model, information related to the topic is retrieved from memory and subjected to various tests of appropriateness. These could be minimal tests of whether the retrieved information "sounds right" in relation to the assignment, or they could be more involved tests in accord with scientific principles. If this piece of information passes the tests, it is entered into notes or text, and the process is repeated to produce more text. Taken out of context, the second and third sentences in the example on the kinetic theory of gases fall within this framework. The second sentence is about motion of particles in a box. It passes the test of relevance to the kinetic theory of molecules. The next cycle concerning particles in a box related to the kinetic theory of motion adds the new cues: particles in a box. The kinetic theory of gases supplies the notion of motion. Subsequent sentences in the first paragraph relate to particles. Content generation and writing continue in this manner until the assignment is completed.

Figure 2.1 is a diagram of the knowledge telling model based on the work of Bereiter and Scardamalia (1987). They note that production of text in this manner permits an immature writer to get started almost immediately and produce text on any reasonable specification of topic. "It preserves the straight-ahead form of oral language production and requires no significant amount of planning or goal setting than does ordinary conversation" (pp. 9–10).

FIGURE 2.1

The Knowledge Telling Model

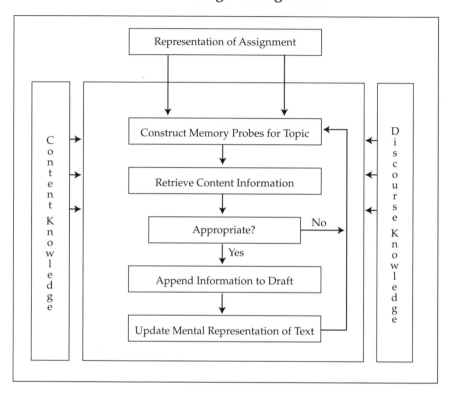

Bereiter and Scardamalia also present a more sophisticated model of writing that is closely related to reflective writing. However, before discussing that model, think about how Abraham Pais, a theoretical physicist and author of a series of books on scientists and their works, approaches writing tasks. Pais (1997), who also wrote roughly 150 research papers, points out that writing books is very different from writing a research paper.

> For a typical theoretical paper: Start a section 1, called Introduction, in the following way: It has been observed [or pointed out that]. . . . Early analyses of these phenomena [slew of references] had led to the conclusion that. . . . In the light of the more recent data it appears, however, that these previous

results need to be extended [or modified or revised].
It is the purpose of the present paper to do so.

In section 2 we summarize previous answers. In
section 3 we introduce the following new feature...
and leave a number of more technical points for an
appendix. In section 4 we summarize our conclusions and present a further outlook. (pp. 429–430)

For his books, Pais used a different approach:

First I make a scribble, writing down things as they
come to mind, correcting and changing things
around... the pages go into a drawer for a month...
then I go back to the scribble... thinking over every
sentence, every word as I go along. Again the pages
go into a drawer, now maybe only for a week. Having done that, I have a draft, which in my experience is final at the 90 percent level. (p. 430)

*Take a moment to think about Pais's approach to writing a book
chapter. In what way does it differ from the knowledge telling model
found in Figure 2.1?*

The book-writing process described by Pais begins with a
freewrite of everything that comes to mind on the topic. Then gradually, after a great deal of thinking and restating, fully formed
thoughts emerge. This is the process that Bereiter and Scardamalia
call knowledge transforming—a model very different from the
knowledge telling model.

The freewrite of everything that comes to mind is the type of
writing found in the first paragraph of the example on the kinetic
theory of gases discussed earlier. The emerging, fully formed
thoughts are like the second paragraph of the freewrite on the kinetic theory of gases. The first paragraph is a sequence of thoughts
related to the topic of kinetic theory of gases, but often one sentence doesn't seem to flow from another. The second paragraph
does not flow easily out of the first. It is a rethinking of the material gathered in the first paragraph. This is no simple edit of the
thoughts that occurred in the first paragraph but a careful reconsideration of what the student wants to say. It is a metacognitive

look at the material. In the knowledge telling model, information on content is retrieved from memory ("Content Knowledge" in Figure 2.1) and structured according to the rules of essay writing ("Discourse Knowledge" in Figure 2.1). Unlike the knowledge telling model, the writing in the freewrite is used to examine the content. That is, the processing of the writing (discourse processing) is actively engaged to examine the content. As the content is processed, the concepts are clarified. New connections are established between the concepts and previous knowledge.

Objectives of the Reflective Writing Activity

Reflective writing helps students to sort out how much they understand about concepts before the class starts and to use the class as an opportunity to try and understand the concepts while the professor is available as a source of expertise. In addition, it helps students to critically examine their ideas about the material presented in the course and in general to improve their critical thinking skills.

Reflective writing liberates students to get to ideas. Peter Elbow (1998) put it this way:

> Schooling makes us obsessed with the "mistakes" we make in writing.... But it's not just "mistakes" or "bad writing" we edit as we write. We also edit unacceptable thoughts and feelings, as we do in speaking. In writing there is more time to do it so the editing is heavier: when speaking, there's someone there waiting for a reply and he'll get bored or think we're crazy if we don't come up with *something*. Most of the time in speaking, we settle for the catch-as-catch-can way in which words tumble out. (p. 5)

A similar experience happens during reflective writing. As students freewrite, they no longer censor their thoughts and instead explore ideas. As their writing leads them into the discovery of their own questions and solutions, students reduce the paralysis of apprehension.

Be certain that students are doing reflective writing, not summary writing. A strategy such as summarizing science/engineering textual material falls into the Bereiter and Scardamalia knowledge telling model rather than the knowledge transforming model. The knowledge telling model, unlike the knowledge transforming model, does not foster the generation of new knowledge because it relies on established connections between content elements and readily available discourse knowledge. If students like to summarize, they should do so before they begin reflective writing.

Getting Students to Read Material in the Textbook Before Coming to Class

The most important use of reflective writing in science courses is to get students to read and metacognitively examine the material in their textbooks to be covered in class that week. To promote metacognitive activity during reflective writing, students should read each portion of the material very carefully before commencing reflective writing, using whatever techniques they are comfortable with to discover the concepts found in the section: underling, highlighting, and/or summarizing. Having established what concepts occur in the section, they are ready to begin reflective writing.

Studying a science/engineering textbook for understanding is often difficult for students due to the gap between prior knowledge and the conceptual knowledge demands of the subject matter domain itself. Other obstacles include the density of concepts presented in the textbook, the typical level of abstraction of scientific/engineering phenomena as one moves away from intuitions based on personal experience, and the strategic demands on students to make sense of the content and solve problems. Consequently, students normally don't read the textbook in conjunction with classroom activities, but rather use it as an adjunct to help solve problems, picking out what they perceive to be useful solved problems and pieces of information.

If students would read the textbook, they would be introduced to the hierarchical nature of the discipline (Van Dijk & Kintsch, 1983). Students require a tool they can use to navigate through the textbook in preparation for classroom activities. Ideally, they would develop questions about the material that would serve as memory markers so they can pick up information from the class that assists them in constructing their understanding of the conceptual underpinnings of the discipline.

Reflective writing can be used to explore the conceptual content presented in the textbook. Students should be active participants in processing the conceptual content of the required textbook reading for each class. Part of what they must do to be successful in constructing meaning is to relate their prior knowledge to the new concepts presented in the text.

How to Do Reflective Writing

It is very important to explain to students how to do reflective writing. In the first class in the course, I usually briefly go over the description of this activity found in my course outline. Then I review it again in detail once the course change period is over. I inform the students that during the class, I will assume that they have read the assigned material. Some of the material and problems found in the text in these readings will not be covered in class, but the exam will be based on everything found in these readings. I assume that students can read and understand the simpler points. If, contrary to my expectations, students have a problem with some concept in their reading that I do not discuss in class, I would expect students to ask about it in class. This gives me extra time to cover more in-class problems, and/or do demonstrations, and/or do other activities in class such as small-group activities.

The following are the instructions that I give to the students:

- Read each section (or two sections if one of the sections is short); carefully focus on what you don't understand and on all points that you would like to be clarified.

- During your reading, use whatever techniques you usually use to understand required reading, including underlining, highlighting, summarizing, and rereading.

- After completing this task, freewrite about what you have read (about two-thirds of a page per section).

- Reflective writing is not essay writing. You will not usually use capitals and will often write fragments of sentences. If at any time you feel that you can't go on—your mind is a blank—write a "nonsense" word over and over, for example, the last word that you wrote, wrote, wrote, wrote . . . until you start writing again.

- Write about the section(s) that you have read. Write about what it means. Try to find out what you don't know and try to understand through your writing the material you don't know. When you are finished, you will be prepared to ask questions in class about all the points that you don't understand.

Students should complete only one section at a time. Suggest they use their time wisely by doing the various sections at different times during the week. For example, if they find they are having difficulties completing a problem assignment in another science/engineering course, they can take a break by reflective writing on a section of their textbook.

When students read a section and underline, highlight, summarize, or reread the section, they usually think they understood the section. But after they do reflective writing, they realize there are points they did not understand and they are prepared for class. They know what questions need to be answered in class. If the professor does not supply the answers, they will ask questions to complete their knowledge of the subject.

The Knowledge Transformation Model

Let's look at the instructions in terms of Figure 2.2. The top two boxes in the figure indicate the setting up of the reflective writing assignment by the student. The two columns on each side of the figure show the two axes that students utilize to examine the material presented in a section of their textbook, namely content knowledge and discourse knowledge. Reflective writing on a section of a textbook is shown in this figure to be an interaction between the student's two knowledge axes. As a student reads a new section and identifies new concepts, the student enhances the content knowledge axis. This information is translated as the student freewrites, enhancing the student's scientific genre knowledge. This leads to an identification of which concepts are clear and which concepts are not. After an examination of the meaning of the concepts, the growth in the student's discourse knowledge axis results in a re-translation of the information so that the student can relate the new content knowledge to previous sections of the textbook. The student is now clear about what information needs to be provided in class to have a full understanding of the material presented in the section. In summary, the processing of the writing (discourse processing) is actively engaged to examine the content. As the content is processed, the concepts are clarified. New connections are established between the concepts and previous knowledge.

FIGURE 2.2
The Knowledge Transformation Model

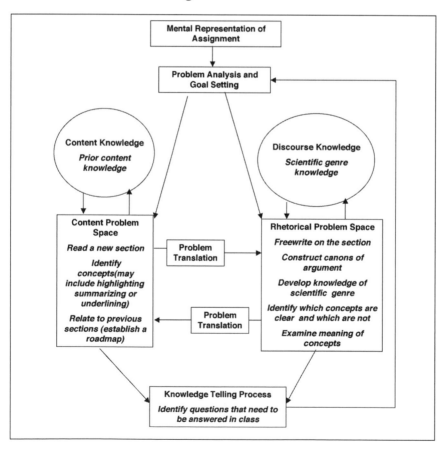

Student Example of Reflective Writing

The overall benefits of the reflective writing process in the context of studying the science/engineering textbook are that it is dynamic, aids understanding, and includes careful reading of the required text before initiating reflective writing. This correlates with what would be predicted by Bereiter and Scardamalia's knowledge transforming model. The following shows a student's progress toward understanding of a concept using the reflective writing process

> *Connecting current and prior textual material.*
> I suppose I should make the meaning of a projectile motion clear in my head. . . . I guess a projectile is an object moving freely under the influence of gravity alone. I don't really understand but I think something about the air resistance being negligible was mentioned. I'm going to back up my statement with an example. Let's assume we want to look at the projectile motion of a ball. To find details about the motion at certain instants, we have to take into account the horizontal and the vertical components. I also have to know several formulas for finding components of velocity of a certain particle. But all of those formulas could be derived from the basic formulas for constant velocity and acceleration that we studied before.

> *Self-checking of conceptual material.*
> I was surprised to read that even though an object would maintain constant velocity it would accelerate, but it doesn't make sense because if the object is not speeding and is traveling at a constant velocity, how would it accelerate? But then I suppose it was explained to me that acceleration depends on the change in the velocity and since velocity is a vector quantity, its magnitude and direction—I forgot to say change in magnitude and direction of velocity—would cause the object to accelerate.

Conceptual clarification.
Let's see if I can get this straight. Acceleration is created when either the magnitude or the direction of the velocity vector is changed.

Marking Reflective Writing

Reflective writing should not be marked for content; students do reflective writing for themselves. If marked, students would write for the instructor, worrying about paragraph and sentence structure.

To make sure that students do reflective writing, different strategies can be employed depending on the size of the class and the nature of the course. In my large introductory courses, I use a method that permits quick marking by TAs, who spend most of the time marking problems. The TA checks to see if the student is on task—that is, writing about the section and freewriting. As long as this is the case, the student receives 100%. If not, points are taken off. The mark for the reflective writing assignment is 5% of their total course mark. In smaller courses, especially those that I grade myself, I ask students to write a preview sheet after doing reflective writing. The preview sheet is only marked if students also hand in the reflective writing. These are the instructions:

> When you have finished the reflective writing on all the sections, reread your jottings and produce a one-page preview of important ideas to be discussed in class that week. The reflective writing will not be marked, but unless you turn in an adequate amount of reflective writing with your preview sheet, the preview sheet will not be marked.

Usually when I require that students write a preview sheet, the concept assignment of reflective writing and preview sheet is worth 20% of the course grade. When TAs mark the assignment, I usually read a small number myself. This has two purposes: 1) I have some idea of the problems the students are having with the material before I see the students in class, and 2) I can use the assignments that I mark for *rangefinding*—checking with the TAs to see that they are giving appropriate marks to the students' assignments.

Student Response to Reflective Writing

I ask students to use reflective writing in all of my courses, from introductory gateway courses through graduate Ph.D.-level courses. In the first few weeks of an introductory science course, students will have difficulties adjusting to nonstop freewriting. One student interviewed in such a course stated, "At the beginning . . . I was writing an essay. . . . I wouldn't write continuously. I used to stop a lot . . . and it took a lot of time for me. Now if I don't understand it when reading, when I write it, it just so happens that I understand it for some reason . . ." These comments illustrate that typically science students in the first few assignments do not perform real reflective writing. They are trying to write essays. To help students adjust, I allow them to drop their three worst grades in their reflective writing assignments.

Reflective writing is also useful in my courses for nonscience students. These students are usually concerned about learning science, and I find that the activity helps make them comfortable. They seem to find the course less threatening and even begin to enjoy it. There is really no difference between science students and nonscience students in their progress with their reflective writing throughout the course. All students have difficulty performing reflective writing at the beginning of the course. They have difficulty with the transition from writing essays to writing rapidly, ignoring all rules of grammar and not stopping for editing. After a few assignments, almost all students have made the transition to doing an effective reflective writing assignment. I always do a midcourse evaluation just before I hand back the midterm examinations. By that time, I always find very high approval ratings for this activity, around the 95% level.

In the next chapter, I will discuss how this activity, along with other modes of writing, can be used to ensure that students are aware of the concepts underlying the topics being discussed, rather than viewing the material as an agglomeration of disembodied facts and formulae to be learned.

Summary

- *Reflective writing is a gathering of thoughts on a chosen topic and then a rethinking of these thoughts to develop knowledge. Reflective writing helps students to increase their conceptual acquisition through the interaction between content processing and discourse processing interactions. According to Bereiter and Scardamalia (1987), this interaction provides the stimulus for reflection in writing. A strategy such as summarizing science/engineering textual material without the reflective writing component falls into the Bereiter and Scardamalia knowledge telling model rather than the knowledge transforming model. The knowledge telling model, unlike the knowledge transforming model, does not foster the generation of new knowledge because it relies on established connections between content elements and readily available discourse knowledge.*

- *Using the reflective writing process, students read a section of the textbook and then freewrite about the concepts found in that section. In freewriting, a student starts writing and keeps writing, quickly without editing. This may be difficult at first, but students who do reflective writing are prepared for class. They know what questions need to be answered in class. If the professor does not supply the answers, they will ask questions to complete their knowledge of the subject. The reflective writing is not marked for content. If marked, students would write for the instructor, worrying about paragraph and sentence structure.*

3

Writing-to-Learn

This chapter discusses several uses of writing-to-learn. These are reflective write-pair-share, the course dossier method, and the end-of-semester conference. Research indicates that students do not concentrate very long during a class if the instructor uses only lecturing—after 20 minutes, many students have ceased to engage with the lecture. Reflective write-pair-share is a good way to break off from the lecture for a short period of time to concentrate on a particularly important concept. The instructor then returns to lecturing. The course dossier method and the end-of-semester conference are ways for students to analyze the important concepts in the course out of the classroom.

Reflective writing is part of the writing-to-learn movement that incorporates informal writing into all disciplines. Using writing to engage the student with the material has long been done in mathematics (see especially Connolly & Vilardi, 1989, and Countryman, 1992. Pugalee, 1997, reviews the various uses of writing in the teaching of mathematics). With some exceptions (Hein, 1994; Kalman & Kalman, 1997; Kirkpatrick & Pittendrigh, 1984; Mullin, 1989a, 1989b), physics and other sciences lagged behind mathematics in employing writing-to-learn techniques.

Rivard (1994) notes that writing as a response is intimately connected to thinking. Here we are not simply referring to writing an essay or report on a science topic. A report on "what they did in a lab or . . . discussion of some topic in the course" leads to rote learning by the student (Barnes, Britton, & Torbe, 1990). In this use of writing, students learn the teacher's expectations and what points should be delivered to the teacher (and ultimately on the exam) rather than engaging with the subject themselves. Such writing falls within Bereiter and Scardamalia's (1987) knowledge telling model described in Chapter 2. Writing in the context of the more robust knowledge transforming model (also found in Chapter 2) in science courses allows students to mediate their own "knowledge" with the new knowledge presented in the course. Writing-to-learn and learning to write explore the student's own doubts, gaps in knowledge, and gropings for the answer. Writing-to-learn activities can be incorporated within the course structure without losing a significant amount of teaching time. As little as 10 minutes of class time on a regular basis (reflective write-pair-share) will add significantly to students' ability to assimilate and think critically about the concepts introduced in class. Alternatively, or additionally, some writing can be incorporated into the course in the form of outside assignments (the course dossier method and the end-of-semester conference).

Writing can help avoid the "dead space" of fear, those times when a student's anxiety blocks his or her ability to think during an exam, to produce a reasoned and competently written paper, or to solve problems efficiently and creatively. Writing-to-learn reduces the paralysis of apprehension and leads students into the discovery of their own questions and solutions. This method helps circumvent attempts by students to regurgitate lecture material and discourages students from simply manipulating the prevailing models and formulae of their disciplines. Writing-to-learn helps students to learn how to learn and to apply what they learn, rather than memorizing what an expert has established. Additionally, writing-to-learn helps students move to higher orders of thinking. Moreover, students can write their way into an understanding of difficult concepts which they have not grasped before.

Elbow (1998) points out that writing is a recursive act that can be viewed as a holistic process involving successive drafts that move unevenly from an imprecise understanding of a text or problem through increasingly more complex, lucid, and coherent interpretations. Through this process, which can take many forms, including the course dossier and reflective write-pair-share exercises, students not only can acquire new knowledge but can come to change the preconceived concepts with which they enter university and which block analytic and interpretive learning.

Reflective Write-Pair-Share

Reflective write-pair-share can be used to break up lectures when student attention begins to wander, to examine salient points in the course in depth, and to permit students to construct their own knowledge throughout the entire course.

Scenario for a Class

How many instructors believe that students do not ask meaningful questions in class? That they are not excited about the subject, and therefore are not exciting to teach? The goal of reflective write-pair-share is to have short, meaningful discussions in class. The way reflective write-pair-share fits into a typical class is shown in Figure 3.1. The discussion is student based, with the instructor acting primarily as chair and resource person.

FIGURE 3.1

Example of Reflective Write-Pair-Share

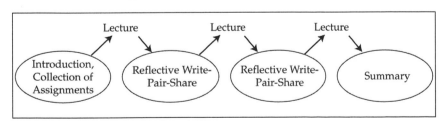

Each discussion should center on a short topic that can be placed on a single transparency. Initially the students engage metacognitively with this material. Next they share their thoughts with a partner, and finally the whole class discusses the topic. You may want to begin with a simple demonstration. For example, take some keys and pick up a piece of paper. Then drop each of them. Crumble the paper, then drop it and the keys again. Then present students with the transparency shown Figure 3.2.

FIGURE 3.2

Typical Transparency

Consider the paper and the keys in both experiments.

- What is involved in the motion in each case?

- Why do the keys and paper react differently in the first experiment?

- What conclusions do you draw from the second experiment?

Students read the transparency and some may write notes or summarize its contents. Next they use reflective writing for a short, fixed time (the amount of time depends on the content displayed on the transparency, but not more than five minutes) to examine the conceptual underpinnings of the material.

After completing their reflective writing on the topic or demonstration, students share their ideas with a partner, then the discussion is opened up to the entire class.

The Course Dossier Method

Science is not composed simply of equations and of problems to solve. Many, if not most, undergraduate students think that science is nothing more than a tool box of techniques to be used to deal with particular issues. To understand real science, they need to deal with concepts. Writing can be used to ensure that students are aware of the concepts underlying the topics being discussed, rather than viewing the material as an agglomeration of disembodied facts and formulae to be learned. The course dossier method takes students beyond the reflective writing on the textbook discussed in

Chapter 2 to using writing to explore critically the material presented in class. I have used this method in the most advanced undergraduate physics courses and in science courses designed for nonscience students.

The full course dossier method begins with students writing one-page preview sheets (reflections) of material to be discussed in class each week and one-page critiques of concepts that were discussed in class each week. At the end of the course, students write a final essay about the development of some themes that occurred throughout the course. They use their collection of critiques to help find the themes. In many courses, it is desirable to have students write reflections and critiques, but it is impractical to have them write a final essay. This truncated version of the course dossier method without the final essay is called the mini-research paper method.

Transforming Each Lecture Into a Mini-Research Paper

Winner of the 1992 Bright Ideas Award of the Society for Teaching and Learning in Higher Education, the mini-research paper asks students to prepare one-page preview sheets (reflections) prior to the week's classes. The reflection is the equivalent of the planning phase of an essay. The lecture then becomes the research component, the material to be addressed. A one-page postsummary (critique) is the body of the research.

Before writing their reflection, students should perform reflective writing on the material to be covered in class in the coming week. (This is the same reflective writing activity described in Chapter 2.) After rereading their reflective writing, they write the one-page reflection.

At the top of the reflection, students write two or three mini-objectives that they think should be addressed in class that week. For the remaining one-page reflection, students write a summary of *all* the topics to be covered in the coming week. The reflections are not marked unless students submit an adequate amount of reflective writing with the reflections. The reflective writing is not marked.

The critique may take various forms. In a regular science course, it would consist of a short introductory paragraph followed by a presentation of what was covered in the week's classes. In a course for nonscience students, it would be a one-page essay, written in a manner that anyone could understand. This essay would begin with a short introductory paragraph about one concept presented in class that week. The rest of the essay would be a critical analysis of the concept. In either case, students are warned that critiques must be presented in properly written paragraphs using normal writing or 12-point font and as few equations as possible. Points are deducted for unnecessary use of mathematics and extra pages are not read.

Students at all levels tend to think that science consists of laws and equations. They do not look for the ideas and themes that comprise the subject. By writing about mini-objectives in the reflection and critiquing a concept after material is covered in class, students grasp the ideas underpinning the subject.

End of Semester

In courses for nonscience students and in smaller upper-year courses, the set of mini-research papers can be enhanced by a fuller recursive and interactive approach to writing. At the end of the course, the students collect all or a sample of their critiques and write a single overview of the course using the following procedure:

- *First entries:* Two friends who are not in the course read the collected critiques and make comments.

- *Second entries*: The student rereads the collected critiques with the comments and writes reflectively on the collection.

- *Third entries:* The second entries are used to develop a common theme(s) that runs through the work.

- *Fourth entries:* The themes are developed into a draft of an essay of n pages. (For an upper-year science course, this n would likely be 3 pages. For a nonscience course with a final exam, 5 pages. For such a nonscience course where the dossier is in place of a final exam, 10 pages.) The essay must be a critical examination *covering* the entire course in terms of the themes based on material discussed in class.

- *Fifth entries:* The two friends read the draft and record their comments.

- *Final entries:* The draft is rewritten reflecting a reconsideration of the material, especially in light of the remarks by the two friends. Suggested length n pages, but there is no page limit.

Students are informed that if any entry is missing from the dossier, the dossier will not be marked. Since grading a course dossier takes time, it is not practical to use this method in a large class with an additional final examination. Thus for science courses, I confine the use of the full course dossier method to small upper-year courses. I usually employ the truncated mini-research paper method or reflective writing alone instead of the full course dossier method in larger science courses. In nonscience courses, I use the course dossier method instead of a traditional final examination. Nonscience students relate well to the course dossier method and learn more about what science is and how it works through this method. They cover the content in their reflections and critiques.

"In order for reflection to occur, the oral and written forms of language must pass back and forth between persons who both speak and listen or read and write—sharing, expanding, and reflecting on each other's experiences" (Belenkey, Clinchy, Goldberger, & Tarule 1997, p. 26). Prewriting, drafting, and rewriting are integral to any successful piece of writing; what is often overlooked is that one never can "get it right" in the first draft. Writing is a recursive process, one that goes backward and forward and backward again, from noting initial conceptions to drafting the work to regeneration of new ideas and new formats. The course dossier provides ample opportunity for all of this. Note that the passing of the draft to the two friends not only provides feedback, but also forces the student to establish distance from the material before writing the final version.

Students in upper-year courses become proficient at doing science, but they usually do not clearly understand the concepts. The course dossier method helps advanced students value the course writing assignments and allows them to develop as critical thinkers. The following comments, from a student originally from Columbia and whose first language was not English, underscores this.

> The post-summaries and the post post-summary (the course dossier) . . . served two purposes. They allowed us to think about what had been presented in a critical manner and they made us translate our thoughts to paper in a clear manner. I believe that these two items can't be separated from each other. It doesn't matter how well one understands the material if one is not able to transmit the "digested" ideas. I don't think that one could present ideas clearly without a thorough understanding of such ideas; so in a sense I think that the two items are really one.

> Once again, during the nearly four years of courses at the university, I had so little opportunity to try to express the ideas covered that the only problem that I see with the course dossier method is that it should have been introduced to us from the beginning. Physics is a beautiful and profound subject but most of my courses dealt with the mathematical formulation and with solving problems. Due to this lack of wrapping up, I feel that my knowledge in some fields could have been greatly increased if I had had time to translate this mathematical language and apparently unrelated ideas into a coherent and structured "all."

Students need to understand concepts in science and not be trained only in techniques. An intervention such as the course dossier method is thus a vital part of the education of a scientist. For the nonscientist, a scheme such as the course dossier method is also needed so that students can appreciate how science works. The next section presents another writing-to-learn method that is an alternate to the course dossier method: the end-of-semester conference. This method might be a better approach for non-science students for it gives students the idea of how a scientific conference functions.

Hosting an End-of-Semester Conference

Larkin-Hein and Budny (2001) discuss courses where students are asked to prepare and present a professional research paper for a "conference." Early in the semester, students are informed that one of the key components of the course will be the preparation of a formal written paper for publication and presentation at a conference to be held at the end of the term. The goal is to have students explore a topic or topics in more depth than is covered in class, thus making them the "experts." Throughout the semester, students are exposed to all aspects involved in the preparation of a formal paper for publication, including responding to a call for papers, being notified of the acceptance of their abstracts, conducting the necessary research, preparing and submitting a paper for review, conducting a review, and receiving and using the feedback to prepare a final paper. The process of writing the paper and then receiving a review is part of the same recursive process utilized in the course dossier method that makes the end-of-semester conference an effective writing-to-learn method.

The conference call for papers is distributed at the beginning of the semester. Students receive a paper copy as well as an electronic copy of the call via the class listserv and web page. This call is an incentive for students to choose a topic for their papers early. Many students find it challenging to effectively summarize a paper they have not yet written in a 150-word abstract. Writing this abstract requires students to look at the big picture. Approximately one week after the submission of their abstracts, students are informed (electronically) that either their abstract has been accepted or it needs to be revised because the initial topic does not parallel the conference theme closely enough. See Figure 3.3 for a sample call for papers for the 2005 New Millennium Conference at American University.

When students receive notification that their abstracts are accepted, they also receive a copy of the formatting guidelines to be followed as they prepare their papers. Typically, the guidelines given to students are the same as the guidelines given to authors submitting a paper to an education conference (typical guidelines are found in Appendix 3.1). Students are also given a copy of a

FIGURE 3.3

New Millennium Conference

5th Annual New Millennium Conference
April 22, 2005
CALL FOR PAPERS

Abstracts are now being accepted for the *New Millennium Conference* to be held from approximately 12:45 p.m.–5:00 p.m. on Friday, April 22, 2005, at American University in Washington, DC. A wide range of paper topics will be considered. Where possible, papers should involve some aspect of the topics listed on the Physics for the New Millennium course syllabus (sound and waves, electricity and magnetism, light and color, and modern physics/quantum mechanics).

Possible presentation/paper topics include (but are not limited to):

- Historical, current, or futuristic views on a topic related to sound, waves, electricity, magnetism, light, color, or quantum mechanics
- Physics as it relates to the design, development, and/or function of a commonly used device (e.g., What is the physics involved in a burglar alarm? How is sound created for a film? How does the detector in the light meter of a camera work? How does an airport security scanner work? How does an electrostatic precipitator work?)
- Physics/science and public policy issues
- Physics/science and society issues
- Medical applications of physics
- Physics as it relates to any major offered by American University
- Other topics of broad interest

All topics must be cleared with the conference coordinator. The deadline for submission of abstracts is Tuesday, January 25, 2005. Authors will be notified as to the acceptance of their abstracts on or before Tuesday, February 1, 2005. Please note that first drafts of papers will be due on Friday, February 25, 2005. Final drafts of papers are due on Tuesday, March 22, 2005. "Camera ready" copies are due on Friday, April 15, 2005. Note: These are *firm* deadlines.

All submissions will be done electronically. Abstracts should be limited to 200 words. To submit your abstract go to http://fie.engrng.pitt.edu/phys200/Abstract and follow the links.

Please direct all questions and correspondence to:
Dr. Teresa Larkin, Conference Coordinator
Department of Computer Science, Audio Technology, and Physics
4400 Massachusetts Avenue, NW
Washington, DC 20016–8058
tlarkin@american.edu
202-885-2766

Note. Reprinted with permission of Teresa Larkin.

paper written for such a conference. All students' papers are subjected to a formal review process, usually by a faculty member and a student. Papers that need substantial revision must be resubmitted for further review. Most papers range in length from five to eight formatted pages.

At American University, a spiral-bound conference proceeding was produced and distributed to each student on the day of the conference (see Appendix 3.2). The students prepared and made use of overhead transparencies, PowerPoint slides, and demonstrations during their presentations. They were given 10 minutes for their presentations and then allowed 2 minutes for questions. Students were requested to wear appropriate attire for the conference.

Attendance at such a conference is usually restricted to members of the class. If feasible, it may be more effective to open the conference to other members of the college or university. It is important to note that the paper preparation activity was initially designed with nonmajors in mind. However, this writing activity could easily be applied to other courses in science and engineering, both for majors as well as nonmajors, as was indeed done with freshman engineers at the University of Pittsburgh.

Summary

- *Writing-to-learn activities can be incorporated into the course structure without losing a significant amount of teaching time.*

Reflective Write-Pair-Share

- *Discuss a short topic that can be placed on a single transparency.*

- *Students read the transparency and write notes or summarize its contents.*

- *Students use reflective writing for a short, fixed time to examine the content's conceptual underpinnings.*

- *Students share their ideas with a partner.*

- *Discussion is opened to the whole class.*

The Course Dossier Method

The Mini-Research Paper Method

- *Students prepare preview sheets prior to the week's classes (the equivalent to the planning phase of an essay).*

- *Class lecture becomes the research component, the material to be addressed.*

- *A one-page critique is the body of the research.*

The Mini-Research Paper Method as the First Part of a Course Dossier

- *In courses for nonscience students and in smaller upper-year courses, the mini-research paper method can be extended by a fuller recursive and interactive approach to writing based on a series of written entries. If any entry is missing from the dossier, the dossier will not be marked.*

End-of-Semester Conference

- *A key component of the course is the preparation of a formal written paper for publication and presentation at an end-of-term conference.*

- *Students explore a topic(s) in more depth, thus making them the "experts."*

- *Students' papers undergo a formal review process, usually from a faculty member and a student.*

- *A spiral-bound conference proceeding is produced and distributed to each student on the day of the conference.*

- *Students have 10 minutes for their presentations and 2 minutes for questions.*

Appendix 3.1

Preparation of Papers in Two-Column Format
for the 5th Annual New Millennium Conference

Teresa L. Larkin[1]

Abstract—All papers must include an abstract with the submission. The abstract and index terms text should be 10 point, Times New Roman, italics, full justified, and contained within one paragraph. Begin the abstract with the word Abstract—*in Times New Roman, italic,* **Bold** *text, only the word* **Abstract** *should be bolded. Do not indent. Use an "em dash" after the words Abstract and Index Terms. The em dash can be found in the "Insert" menu. From there, select "Symbol" and click on the "Special Characters" tab. Do not cite references in the abstract. The abstract should be no more than 200 words in length. This example abstract is 129 words. Avoid using abbreviations in the abstract. If abbreviations are unavoidable, write their meaning in the abstract.*

***Index Terms**—About four key words or phrases, in alphabetical order, separated by commas (e.g., Camera ready, new millennium, preparation of papers, two-column format).*

Page Layout

These instructions serve as a template for Microsoft Word and give you the basic guidelines for preparing camera-ready papers for the 5th Annual New Millennium Conference to be held in Washington, DC, on April 22, 2005. Please carefully follow the instructions provided in these guidelines to ensure legibility and uniformity. The guidelines were designed to reduce the amount of white space and maximize the amount of text that can be placed on one page.

When you open these guidelines electronically, select "Print Layout" from the "View" menu (View | Print Layout), which will allow you to see the two-column format and the footnote. You may then type over sections using the cut and paste commands (Edit | Paste) into this document and/or by using the markup styles. The pull-down style menu is at the left of the Formatting Toolbar at the top of your Word window (e.g., the style at this point in the document is "Body Text"). To use these built-in style guides, highlight a section that you want to designate with a certain style, and then select the appropriate name on the style pull-down menu.

All papers must adhere to the following layout:

- 8.5" x 11" paper size

- Portrait orientation

- Two-column format for the body of the document

- Top and bottom margins: 1.0"

- Spacing between columns: 0.2"

- Column width: 3.4"

- Indents: first paragraph of section, none;
  all other paragraphs, 0.25"

- Column width: 3.4"

- Indents: first paragraph of section, none;
  all other paragraphs, 0.25"

Set the margin widths and paper size from the "File" menu by selecting "Page Setup." Select the above options and make sure you also apply to "Whole document."

While formatting your document, make consistent use of punctuation marks and spelling. There are two basic systems used by American and British authors. Either American or British is acceptable, but it must be consistent (i.e., not a mix). For example,

- Putting commas and periods outside of quotation marks (e.g., ", and ". instead of ," and ." The latter is American usage and the former is British.

- Use of single quotes (e.g., 'service center' (British) rather than "service center" (American).

- Text such as "grey" and "disc" (British) vs. "gray" and "disk" (American).

Paper Title and Author Data

The title and author data is in one-column format, while the rest of the paper is in two-column format. To accomplish this, most word processors have a section break that is installed to separate the one and two-column format. It is suggested that you open a new document and begin by inserting the title and author information in the standard one-column format and then inserting a section break to begin the body of the paper. Please adhere to the following style guidelines:

- **Paper title:** This information should be placed at the top of the first page in 14 point, Times New Roman, UPPERCASE, **bold**, and centered. This style is defined under the style menu of this document as "TITLE."

- **Author listing:** 12 point, Times New Roman, *italic*, centered. This style is defined under the style menu of this document as "Author."

- Insert a blank line between the title and the author listing and between the author listing and the body of the paper.

Include only the author name in the author listing. Use the full first name for the author. Information for each author, such as email, department or college, university, city, state, and zip, will be listed as a footnote.

- **The footnote text** should be 8 point, Times New Roman, full justified, no space between the paragraphs. This style is defined under the style menu of this document as "Footnote text."

This is the only footnote allowed in the paper. To insert a footnote in Word, place the curser at the end of the name and select the "Insert" menu and then select "footnote" using the bottom of the page and auto numbering options.

Paper Body Format

The following information is for a "Full Paper" format. Every presentation at the conference must have a peer-reviewed paper submission.

Column Format Instructions

The title and author data is in one-column format, while the rest of the paper is in two-column format. To accomplish this, most word processors have a section break that is installed to separate the one and two-column format. For example, in Word, under the "Insert" menu select "Section Break" with the "Continuous" option.

After you enter the title and author information, enter a few blank lines and then insert a section break. Now you must define this section to be in two-column format. To do this in Word, under the "Format" menu select "Columns." This option will have an input box for the number of columns. Enter 2 and then set the spacing to 0.2". If you have the margin widths set correctly, the width of the column should display as 3.40". If it does not, go to the "File" menu and select "Page Setup." This will open an input box that will allow you to set the top and bottom margins to 1" and the right and left margins to 0.75". Every word processor will have its own method of accomplishing the above; however, most follow the same format.

Note that the new version of Word has problems when it tries to insert the footnote from the one-column top section below the two-column section. Thus, in many cases it breaks the text and puts the title and author listing on a separate page. If you have this new "improved" version of Microsoft Word and have this problem, your best option is to simply use this document as a template and cut and paste your own paper over the text in these guidelines.

Font and Spacing Instructions

Use the full justify option for your columns, and use two-columns in all pages. The two columns must always exhibit equal lengths and you should try to fill your last page as much as possible. To obtain such results, you are free to adjust the figure sizes, provided this does not compromise their clarity. Use one line of space between text and section headings. Use one line of space between text and captions, equations, tables, and footnote. Use the spelling and grammar checkers. Do not use the "hyphenation" feature in Word. Please use the following font and alignment instructions:

- **Body text:** 10 point, Times New Roman, full justified, single space, no blank lines between the paragraphs. Indents: first paragraph of section, none (this style is defined under the style menu of this document as "First Paragraph"). Indent: all other paragraphs, 0.25" (this style is defined under the style menu of this document as "Body Text"). Follow the examples shown in this document.

- **Section headings:** 12 point, Times New Roman, **bold**, centered. Use SMALL CAPS, leaving one blank line above and below. For example, "Page Layout" on page one of this document is a Section Heading (this style is defined under the style menu of this document as "Section Headings").

- **Section sub-headings:** 10 point, Times New Roman, **bold**, centered. Leave one blank line above and below. For example, "Font and Spacing Instructions" on this page is a Section Sub-heading (this style is defined under the style menu of this document as "Subheading").

- **Bullets:** 10 point, Times New Roman, left justify, indent text 0.25". Insert a blank line after the bulleted list, but not before; follow the examples in this document (this style is defined under the style menu of this document as "Bullets").

Page Numbering

Do not put page numbers on your manuscript. Page numbers will automatically be added by the conference coordinator in conjunction with the publication of the conference proceedings.

Figures, Tables, and Equations

All figures and tables must fit either one- or two-column width, 3.4" or 7" wide respectively. It is suggested that you use the two-column format whenever possible. If your table or figure will not fit into one of the two columns on the page, then insert a continuous section break before and after the table or figure, as described above, and define it as one column. To make the paper easier to read, you may want to position any table or figure that requires one column either at the bottom of the page or at the top of a new page.

Do not abbreviate "Table." Use Roman numerals to number tables. Use the following formatting guidelines for figures and tables:

- **Figure and table headings:** 10 point, Times New Roman, UPPERCASE, centered. Place below the figure and above the table (this style is defined under the style menu of this document as "Figure Heading").

- Leave one blank line above and below each table or figure.

- **Figure and table captions:** 8 point, Times New Roman, SMALL CAPS, centered. Place below the figure or table headings (this style is defined under the style menu of this document as "Figure Caption").

Table I and Figure 1 below illustrate the proper table and figure formatting. Avoid placing figures and tables before their first mention in the text. When inserting figures or tables be sure you insert the figure and not just a link to the figure. The best way to make sure you are doing this correctly is to save your paper to a floppy disk then open the file on a different machine and make sure all your figures are correct. If you insert the link instead of the figure or table, a box with a big red X will appear in the location where the table or figure is supposed to be placed.

TABLE I

Point Sizes and Type Styles

Points	Place of Text	Type Styles
10	Table number	ROMAN NUMERALS
10	Figure and table headings	UPPERCASE
8	Figure and table captions	SMALL CAPS
8	Footnote	
8	Reference list	
10	Footer	**Bold**
10	Abstract and index terms	*Italics*
12	Section titles	SMALL CAPS, **Bold**
10	Main text and equations	
10	Subheadings	**Bold**
12	Authors' names	*Italics*
14	Title	UPPERCASE, Bold

FIGURE 1

Logo of the Institute for Electrical and Electronics Engineers

Number equations in parenthesis flush with the right margin,

$$2jk\ \partial u/\partial z = \partial^2 u/\partial x^2 + k^2\ (n^2 - \beta^2)\ u \tag{1}$$

Refer to "(1)," not "Eq. (1)" or "Equation (1)," except at the beginning of a sentence: "Equation (1) is . . ."

Headers and Footers

Please use the following format guidelines for the Header and Footer:

- **Header text:** should say Session as shown on the top of this document. Text should be 14 point, Times New Roman, right justified, **bold** (this style is defined under the style menu of this document as "Header").

- **Footer text:** 10 point, Times New Roman, **bold** (this style is defined under the style menu of this document as "Footer"). The text of the footer should be the same as shown on the bottom of this document. Please copy and paste this information into your document exactly as shown on this page.

Acknowledgment

The preferred spelling of the word "acknowledgment" in American English is without an "e" after the "g." Use the singular heading even if you have many acknowledgments. Put sponsor acknowledgments in an unnumbered footnote on the first page.

References

Place references in a separate section at the end of the document. Do not footnote references. Refer simply to the reference number, as [3] or [5]–[8]. Do not use "Ref. [3]" or "reference [3]" except at the beginning of a sentence (for example, "Reference [3] shows . . ."). Provide up to five authors' names; replace the others by "et al." Do not put figures or anything else after the references.

- **Reference text:** 8 point, Times New Roman, full justified, no space between the references (this style is defined under the style menu of this document as "References").

- Use box numbers with square brackets [ ] within the text. Do not use superscripts or subscripts. Do not use parentheses ( ) for references, since these are used to refer to equations.

Use the following as the guide for references:

- Author's Last Name, First Initial, Middle Initial, "Title," *Journal or book*, Vol. No., date, pp.

[1] Teresa L. Larkin, American University, Department of Computer Science, Audio Technology, and Physics, 4400 Massachusetts Avenue, NW, Washington, DC 20016–8058, tlarkin@american.edu

APPENDIX 3.2

Physics for a New Millennium Conference

April 26, 2002
1:15 p.m.–5:00 p.m.
McKinley Hall, Room 108

Moderator:
Dr. Teresa L. Larkin

The Third Annual New Millennium Conference will feature presentations by a number of speakers on cutting edge topics in physics. The conference will consist of five sessions:

I. Conference Welcome

II. A Potpourri of Physics

III. Innovations in Sound I

IV. Innovations in Sound II

V. Technology in the New Millennium

In addition to presentations that utilize various aspects of physics, several of the featured speakers will share the historical underpinnings related to their specific topics. Speakers will also provide a look at what the future of the technology may be as we move into the next millennium.

Read on for a detailed view of the conference program.

SESSION I: CONFERENCE WELCOME

Presentation 1: 1:15 p.m.–1:25 p.m.
The Importance of Physics in the New Millennium
Invited Speaker: Larry Medsker

SESSION II: A POTPOURRI OF PHYSICS

Presentation 1: 1:30 p.m.–1:42 p.m.
From Edison's Patent to Your Lamp: An Engineering Journey
Author: Tara S. Ormond

Presentation 2: 1:42 p.m.–1:54 p.m.
The Human Eye: Magic or Simple Science?
Author: Bridget Dooley

Presentation 3: 1:54 p.m.– 2:06 p.m.
The Good and Bad Behind Electromagnetic Fields
Author: Kathryn von Richthofen

SESSION III: INNOVATIONS IN SOUND I

Presentation 1: 2:10 p.m.– 2:22 p.m.
No More Bad Concert Halls
Author: Ryan Luan

Presentation 2: 2:22 p.m.– 2:34 p.m.
The Fascinating World of Architectural Acoustics
Author: Ana M. Cetina

Presentation 3: 2:34 p.m.– 2:46 p.m.
Helping the Deaf to Hear
Author: Erin L. Turner

SESSION IV: INNOVATIONS IN SOUND II

Presentation 1: 3:15 p.m.– 3:27 p.m.
From Electricity to Audio: How Loudspeakers Create Sound
Author: Jeremy A. Luks

Presentation 2: 3:27 p.m.– 3:39 p.m.
Effects Processors: Revolutionizing the World of Sound
Author: Matthew A. Thomas

SESSION V: TECHNOLOGY IN THE NEW MILLENNIUM

Presentation 1: 3:50 p.m.– 4:02 p.m.
Let It Flow
Author: Andrew Meyer

Presentation 2: 4:02 p.m.– 4:14 p.m.
The Computing of Today and Tomorrow
Author: John Lenss

Presentation 3: 4:14 p.m.– 4:26 p.m.
Who's Listening In?
Author: Danielle L. Davis

Presentation 4: 4:26 p.m.– 4:38 p.m.
Credit Card Technology
Author: Andres F. Rodriguez

Presentation 5: 4:38 p.m.– 4:50 p.m.
Electric Vehicles: The Resurrection of Alternative Transportation
Author: James E. Harper

4

Constructing Student Knowledge

Students entering the classroom in an introductory (gateway) science course face many obstacles. One such difficulty is reading and understanding the material as presented in their textbooks. When students examine a section of the textbook using the reflective writing techniques of Chapter 2, they often find that many of the concepts are hard to understand, even though textbooks typically have a deceptively easy language. Even when students think they understand the concept, that understanding is often very different (student alternate scientific conception) from the way scientists understand it.

It is widely recognized that students enter introductory (gateway) science courses with concepts (personal scientific concepts) that are different from those found in the course. In the traditional lecture system, information flows primarily from the professor to the students; information which the students can easily adapt to fit their own system of beliefs about the world. Because a student's understanding differs from the perspective presented in the textbook and delivered by the instructor in the classroom, he or she misreads the textbook and mishears the instructor's words. Half or more of students entering introductory courses have not developed intellectually to the level needed to succeed in the course. In addition to their preconceived ideas about the course content, students are also resistant to changing those ideas. In this chapter, student resistance to understanding the conceptual framework given in the science textbook and in the lecture is discussed. Solutions to overcoming this resistance within the traditional course will be presented in subsequent chapters.

Students' Intellectual Development

Most modern philosophers of science would agree that the demarcation between a science and a pseudo-science like astrology is the use of experimentation and the connection of material within a comprehensive system in scientific subjects.

The efforts of educators since John Dewey have been to develop a systematic approach to education—a *science of pedagogy*—constantly refined by experiment. At the beginning, one can think of classic experiments with children by the Swiss educator Jean Piaget (1929), who presents the concept of stages in students' intellectual development. Certain operations that are "sensible" to older students are not sensible to younger students. Piaget suggests that children go through intellectual changes from one stage of cognition to another several times as they mature.

- Sensory-motor stage
- Preoperational stage (age 1 ½)
- Concrete operational stage (ages 7–11)
- Formal operational stage (age 14 or 15)

Inhelder and Piaget (1958) further divide each of the last two stages into two substages. Before a student is able to think about abstract ideas, children in the concrete operational stage explore their world tactically, experiencing concepts without forming abstract generalizations of their findings. Renner and Paske (1977) illustrate this with the following extract from James Michener's (1975) novel, *Centennial.*

> He was only a peasant, but like all men with seminal ideas, he found the words he needed to express himself. He had heard a professor use the words *imprison* and *replenishment* and he understood immediately what the man meant, *for he ... had discovered the concept before he heard the word* [italics added], but when he did hear it, the word was automatically his, for he had absorbed the idea which entitled him to the symbol. (p. 565)

When concrete operational learners experience a concept and have it labeled for them, they are able to discover its value. Exploration, invention, and discovery represent inquiry and lead the student to what Piaget (1973) has called "intellectual independence."

A student in the concrete operational stage can "assimilate data from concrete experiments and arrange and rearrange them in his head" (Renner & Lawson, 1973, p. 168). Looking at the big picture using inductive and deductive reasoning is beyond such a student. Students who have not progressed beyond this stage are "object bound." They do not relate to verbally stated hypotheses. Students who have reached the formal stage are capable of reasoning with propositions only and do not need to refer to objects. It would seem that students entering postsecondary institutions have made the transition to the formal operational stage, but Renner and Paske (1977) state that "approximately 50% of entering college freshmen are concrete operational. In view of this fact, concrete instruction seems to recommend itself to colleges for the first two years" (p. 859). Similarly, Prigo (1978) notes five studies where "approximately 50% of incoming college students have not reached the intellectual stage of development where they can think abstractly (i.e., scientifically)" (p. 752).

A recent study by Coletta and Phillips (2005) that probed the background of the student population at Loyola Marymount University, Southwestern Louisiana University, University of Minnesota, and Harvard University had similar results to those found in a study of two introductory physics courses at the University of Oklahoma by Renner and Paske (1977). This earlier study presents four generalizations:

1) Students experiencing concrete instruction achieve higher scores on examinations dealing with physics content than students experiencing formal instruction.

2) Concrete instruction promotes students' problem-solving abilities better than formal instruction.

3) Concrete instruction promotes intellectual development at both the concrete and formal levels, while formal instruction advances the intellectual development of only those students who have entered the formal operational stage.

4) Students are happier with concrete instruction than with formal instruction.

These findings are likely the reason why Hewitt (1995) notes that "the professor and the students view solving of problems in a very different way. The professor classifies the problems in terms of concepts, while the students classify them by situations" (p. 85).

Student Misconceptions

Beginning in 1973 with the work of Driver, researchers began to explore the concepts held by pre-university students. Major work begun at the University of Washington–Seattle resulted in the formation of the Physics Education Group in the physics department at the university headed by Lillian C. McDermott. It is significant that this group was not in a faculty of education. Professors were not solely trying to apply education and educational psychology principles to the study of science; they were trying to understand the problems facing students studying physics and develop courses to help them overcome these problems.

McDermott (1984) summarized the research on conceptual understanding in mechanics in the 10 years since Driver. She noted that many of the difficulties that students have are not new to experienced teachers.

> However, this information has generally been in anecdotal form, useful primarily to the instructor

> whose experience it reflects. . . . It is only recently
> that student difficulties in physics have begun to be
> documented in a sufficiently systematic manner for
> drawing generalizations that can be shared. . . .
> There is considerable evidence that they [students'
> personal scientific conceptions] are not readily
> abandoned, but are retained together with the ac-
> cepted scientific view. (pp. 31–32)

This acceptance of new concepts while maintaining old beliefs is
known as *assimilation* (Piaget, 1977). Instruction needed to get students to abandon their misconceptions and accept the concepts
taught in their courses is a process known as *accommodation* (Piaget,
1977). If the learner's current conceptual understanding is sufficient
to explain a new situation, the new concepts are said to be *assimi-
lated* by the learner. If the learner's current conceptual understanding cannot be used by the learner, the learner must revise,
reorganize, or replace his or her ideas, known as *accommodation*.

Posner, Strike, Hewson, and Gertzog (1982) point out that students will cling to their misconceptions because these beliefs make
sense in explaining observations they have made about the physical world, and having taken the effort to construct their private understanding, these same students will not easily relinquish their
original viewpoints.

Work at the university level on correcting students' misconceptions began in earnest after the publication of the seminal work of
Halloun and Hestenes (1985a, 1985b), which produced an instrument referred to as a *mechanics diagnostics test* to examine the initial
knowledge state of college physics students (Halloun & Hestenes,
1985a). They tested more than 1,000 students in college-level introductory physics courses at the University of Arizona. In all the sections that were examined, the mean initial scores on the diagnostic
test were between 51% and 53% for the particular four sections that
featured a calculus-level introductory physics course.

> All of the courses were conducted in a lecture recita-
> tion format: with 3 or 4 hours of lecture and 1 hour
> of recitation each week. The lectures were given by a

professor to classes ranging in size from about 80–230 students. Recitation classes of 25 students or less were conducted by graduate teaching assistants. They were devoted to problem solving. The courses did not include laboratory work, but most students took introductory physics lab courses in parallel with the lectures. (p. 1047)

All sections used the same textbook and covered the same chapters. There was a wide variation in the styles of the professors in the four sections. One was a theoretical physicist who emphasized the conceptual structure of the subject with careful definitions and orderly, logical arguments. The other three were experimental physicists. One incorporated many demonstrations into lectures and strove especially to help students develop "physical intuition." The third professor emphasized problem solving, teaching by example, solving one problem after another. The fourth teacher was teaching the course for the first time. Thus it is surprising to find that the same gain occurred in all the sections (all four sections had pretest scores between 51% and 53%, and all four sections had posttest scores of 64% or 65%). Based on these results, Halloun and Hestenes (1985a) concluded that basic knowledge gain under conventional instruction is independent of the professor.

The Force Concept Inventory (Hestenes, Wells, & Swackhamer, 1992), based on the original Halloun and Hestenes (1985a) instrument, has since been used as a pre- and posttest at many universities throughout the world, ranging from junior colleges to Harvard University. The results have always replicated Halloun and Hestenes's conclusions.

Similar concept inventories have now been developed in other subjects. Anderson, Fisher, and Norman's (2002) "Conceptual Inventory of Natural Selection" (CINS) contains the CINS at the end of the article. Horton (2001) has developed a listing of common misconceptions in chemistry that he makes available on request. See also Roy (1996, 1999) and Schmidt (1997).

Halloun and Hestenes (1985b) concluded that many students have a well-integrated system of beliefs about mechanics that is in conflict with the accepted view. They feel that this system is reminiscent of the medieval system of impetus: A body will continue moving in accord with its initial conditions until the initial force that started it moving is dissipated. An opposing view is found in Hammer (1989, 1994), who shows that some students view physics as weakly connected pieces of information to be separately learned, whereas others view physics as a coherent web of ideas to be tied together. Kalman, Morris, Cottin, and Gordon (1999) note that "up until midway through high school, students can be successful at courses by memorizing *templates* for every situation encountered on an examination. Thus it is *natural* for students to *compartmentalize* their knowledge" (p. S45). That is, they apply different templates to different knowledge subsets. Thus students coming into the course are unlikely to have a coherent, well-defined knowledge of the world.

Evidence for this conclusion is found in Huffman and Heller (1995). They administered the Force Concept Inventory (Hestenes, Wells, & Swackhamer, 1992) based on the original Halloun and Hestenes (1985a) instrument, to 750 university students in a calculus-based introductory physics course. They performed a factor analysis on these results and suggested that an explanation of this factor analysis is that students' personal (alternative) scientific conceptions "are best characterized as loosely organized, ill-defined bits and pieces of knowledge that are dependent upon the specific circumstances in question" (p. 141). A framework for describing and correlating characteristics of weakly organized knowledge systems is given in a detailed paper by diSessa (1993).

Critical Thinking

How can students' misconceptions be changed? One strategy that does not work is attacking the students' misconceptions on a concept-by-concept basis. This cannot break the compartmentalization of their knowledge, and for many students it may not be successful because they are not able intellectually to deal with the instruction. Instead, it is more useful to increase the students' critical thinking skills. Halpern (1997) notes that the "critical" part of critical thinking denotes an evaluation component. . . . **When we think critically, we are evaluating the outcomes of our thought processes**—how good a decision is or how well a problem has to be solved. Critical thinking also involves evaluating the thinking process—the reasoning that went into the conclusion we've arrived at or the kinds of factors considered in making a decision. Critical thinking is also called **directed thinking** because it focuses on a desired outcome. (p. 12)

Postsecondary instruction should include two goals:

1) Increase domain knowledge; that is, students understand some body of knowledge defined by the course content.

2) Increase students' critical thinking skills. Students may be able to expand their store of factual knowledge without understanding the concepts.

We need to help students evaluate their conceptual framework so that they realize that they have compartmentalized their knowledge into templates for every situation. Only then can they adopt a holistic approach and appreciate the conceptual framework of the course. In Chapter 7, ways to help students change their epistemologies to meet this goal will be discussed. In conclusion, here is an example of reflective writing used by a student to critically examine concepts.

Projectile motion is the kind of motion a ball makes when thrown forward. . . . As we saw with vectors, we can project its horizontal and vertical velocities out to the x and y axes, and its magnitude (length) can be found with the aid of trigonometry.

Note that the student begins by establishing links of the current material with mathematical concepts derived in a previous chapter. Continuing with reflective writing, the student discovers that this connection helps to establish an important concept.

A projectile motion can be regarded as the superposition of a free falling body and a body moving with constant velocity.

According to Piaget (1929), this concept would not be developed by a student at the concrete operational intellectual stages of development. Only a student who had arrived at the formal operational intellectual stages of development could separate the projectile into two idealized bodies, one falling freely and the other moving horizontally with constant velocity.

Summary

- *Piaget (1929) suggests that children go through intellectual changes from one stage of cognition to another several times as they mature. The stages are sensory-motor, preoperational (age 1 ½), concrete operational (ages 7–11), and formal operational (age 14 or 15).*

- *Historically, there has been a widespread recognition that students enter introductory (gateway) science courses with concepts (personal scientific concepts) that are different from those found in the course. Their personal scientific concepts are not readily abandoned, but are synthesized with the accepted scientific view. This kind of acceptance of new concepts while maintaining old beliefs is known as* assimilation *(Piaget, 1977).*

- *Students coming into a science course are unlikely to have a coherent, well-defined knowledge of the world. In addition, they are highly resistant to changing their ideas. Attacking students' misconceptions on a concept-by-concept basis will not be successful because many are unable intellectually to deal with the instruction. Students need to evaluate their conceptual framework so they see that they have compartmentalized their knowledge into templates for every situation.*

5

Collaborative Groups

One way of eliciting students' misconceptions is to have them work in small collaborative groups. Research has shown that collaborative learning is more effective in promoting critical thinking than competitive or individual learning strategies (see, for example, Gabbert, Johnson, & Johnson, 1986).

The first reported successful use of collaborative learning at the postsecondary level was for calculus classes (Treisman, 1986). Other examples soon followed; for example, Basili and Sanford (1991) discuss how this approach was used in a chemistry course at a suburban community college, and Posner and Markstein (1994) report on cooperative learning in introductory cell and molecular biology. Vygotsky (1978) considered that interaction with others plays an important role in learning.

Team Work and Group Projects

There are many advantages to having students spend part of their time working together. If small-group work is properly designed, the class atmosphere, cognitive outcomes, and—ultimately—learning will be considerably enhanced. In large introductory courses, students are typically new to the university and may feel somewhat alienated by the large-lecture format. The small-group format removes some of the impersonality of the experience. A lively discussion always seems to follow the first group encounter and often results in students being prepared to ask questions and truly participate in the course.

Working with others provides students opportunities to develop social interaction skills, as well as their leadership and organizational skills. It provides them a chance to network and develop friendships. Students can also be encouraged to take phone numbers and email addresses of other students in the group so that they have someone to contact if they miss any classes.

Group work appeals to students with differing learning styles because they can easily fit the varied activities involved with group work to their own unique learning style. Some students don't like to ask questions or otherwise actively participate in a large class, but often open up in a small group. Group work also helps students develop a better understanding of their peers' expectations, motivational levels, and performance. Generally, students performance is better if a small-group component is incorporated into a course.

Benefits of Team Work

As a rule, before students begin to work in groups, you need to draw their attention to the benefits of team work. Unmotivated students will be more of a liability than an asset to the group and inevitably will affect the team's performance. In addition to the advantages just discussed, McLaughlin (1995) lists the following skills profile developed by the Corporate Council on Education, which highlights that employers seek individuals who can:

- Understand and work within the culture of the group
- Plan and make decisions with others and support the outcomes
- Respect the thoughts and opinions of others in the group
- Exercise "give and take" to achieve group results
- Seek a team approach as appropriate

- Lead when appropriate, mobilizing the group for high performance

When students work in small groups, these skills are practiced and enhanced.

Team Formation

If small groups are used in your class regularly, try to arrange the groups so each contains students of differing abilities. If this is impracticable, a random assignment works well. Try and avoid letting friends, who will shut others out, work together in the same group. Other criteria to consider are: If half the students are science majors and the other half of students are from other disciplines, each team could be required to include as many majors as nonmajors. If it is a course where work experience could benefit learning, students with work experience could be assigned to different groups.

Team Size

To fully benefit from team work, each team should be large enough to have its own dynamics and yet small enough to be manageable. Four or five students is generally ideal. Typically, teams with three or fewer students are too small to generate enough interaction. Teams with more than six students are likely to spend more time dealing with logistical problems than with their assigned tasks.

Team Management

Each team should operate efficiently, and each team member should have a well-defined role. One member could be in charge of liaison with the instructor, another in charge of keeping a log of the team's activities, another responsible for reporting to the class as a whole, and so on.

Team Evaluation

Instructors who use team projects typically issue only one grade for the group. Nonetheless, it is possible to give the individuals within each group somewhat different scores than the group mark. Indeed, research has shown that groups will only function effectively with all members actively contributing to the joint effort if there is some form of individual accountability. To this end, groups should submit regular reports throughout the course. In these reports, individual members should be simultaneously submitting their assessments of themselves and all other group members using a form similar to that shown in Figure 5.1. Such a form can be used to boost the grade of members who have made exceptional contributions to the group effort and, if necessary, lower the grade of those who have been "freeloading." So the rating will not be seen as punitive, inform students that bonus marks will be given for exceptional contributions. If any student is rated by the other group members with consistently low participation for two consecutive assignments, the instructor takes this as a sign of a problem within the group and convenes a meeting with all group members to resolve any difficulties.

Group Development

Students cannot just be thrown in a group and expected to work well together. Although some students may view the group as an opportunity to shine and display their leadership abilities, other students may be shy, possibly concerned about collaborating with strangers, or worried that others will regard their ideas as foolish. Tuckman and Jensen (1977) propose that groups progress through five stages: forming, storming, norming, performing, and terminating. The following is based on their descriptions of these stages.

- *Forming.* At first, interactions between group members are reserved and superficial as group members get acquainted with each other and seek out commonalties that would serve to help them work together.

- *Storming.* The initial congeniality is likely to be replaced by conflict and confrontation within the group. Some members may compete for "group leadership" or "group status." This stage is not actually harmful to the group. Students can hone their skills in clearly expressing their opinions and listening to and evaluating other students' views.

FIGURE 5.1
Peer Evaluation of Group Members

Team Number _____

Section _____

Purpose	To assist the professor in ensuring that the "team component" of each individual's grade reflects each person's contributions to the group project.
Assumption	When a member has contributed to the overall work of the team about the same as the average team member, he or she should receive 100% of the "overall team grade" for the team component of the course.
	When a member has made exceptional contributions to the work of the team (e.g., analytical, organizational. written, investigative, verbal), he or she should receive a higher grade (e.g., 110%, 120% of the team grade).
	Similarly, when a member has been contributing less than other members, he or she should receive a lower grade (e.g., 90%, 80% of the team grade).
	There is no requirement that the overall percentage average 100%. For example, it is possible for one member to receive 110% and the rest of the group to receive 100%.
Instructions	List below the members of your team and indicate what percentage of the team grade you recommend for yourself and for each team member. If you have listed a percentage other than 100% for any team member, *indicate why on the back of this form.* For example, "Group member X did extra research and summarized material of a number of relevant chapters for the group."

Name   **Percentage**

1) (Yourself)_____   _____

2) _____   _____

3) _____   _____

4) _____   _____

5) _____   _____

Note. This figure is based on an evaluation form developed by Bob Schulz of the University of Calgary.

- *Norming.* After the conflicts are resolved, students develop trust in each other. They accept responsibility for the roles assigned to them in the group and clarify the groups' goals in carrying out their task.

- *Performing.* This is a stage of high productivity. The group is highly motivated to achieve its goals.

- *Terminating.* This is typically a short period. By reflecting on their association, students not only celebrate their collaboration, but also come to understand how to enhance future group interactions and learning.

Between the forming and terminating stages, there can be more than one cycle of storming, norming, and performing. This is particularly the case if groups are kept together throughout the course to perform a series of tasks. These stages should also be kept in mind when conflict between group members is reported on the evaluation form. Is the group in a storming phase or does the group require mediation? These stages can apply to the class as a whole, so classbuilding as well as teambuilding activities should be monitored in order to quickly pass through the forming stage.

Classroom Warm-Up Activities

In the forming stage, an atmosphere of trust has to be built in the group. A variety of warm-up activities can help create a climate of openness, mutual acceptance, and commitment. Wright (1995) noted that warm-up activities should be integrated, rooted, relevant, appropriate to the subject matter, take into account the level of students, and consider the intellectual and emotional sensitivities of the class. One that I have used is to ask each group to produce a list of the three most influential scientists that the world has ever known. It is likely that the group members would all have different ideas about whom to put on the list, so they would get used to working together to reach a consensus on a group report. In the process, they also learn about how the other group members function in a group context. Figure 5.2 provides a task sheet of instructions for this assignment.

FIGURE 5.2

Task Sheet

1) Form a group with four others with the same symbol at the bottom of their task sheet.

2) Assign roles to group members: timekeeper, critic, facilitator, recorder, and presenter.

3) Take five minutes to learn the background of the other group members.

4) Your group has five minutes to produce a list of the three most influential scientists that the world has ever seen.

5) Groups will be asked to report on their findings.

✂ or ☎ or ☛ or ✳ or ✈

Ted Panitz (1995) also offers the following warm-ups:

> 1. The Interview—I ask students to pair up with the person next to them and "interview" them or just talk to each other to find out why their new buddy is in school, what they are majoring in, what hobbies or outside interests they have and specifically what is their biggest concern about being in the class. They have 10–15 minutes to accomplish their discussion.
>
> 2. Finding Things In Common—In groups of four I ask them to find five things they all have in common. I chose 5 so that they can't each pick one thing and be finished. The restriction is that they cannot pick school or work items. They must be personal such as what music they like, books they read or travels, etc. They then report back to the whole class their results.

See West (1997) for additional warm-up activities.

Roles for Group Members

If groups are to work effectively together, they need to learn to work as a team and not just as a bunch of individuals. The warm-up activities have begun the process, but the framework for the successful *interdependence* of the group requires more. As noted by Johnson, Johnson, and Smith (1991, pp. 4–9), explicit roles assigned to group members can help.

- *Timekeeper:* In charge of keeping the group on schedule, ensures that the work is completed in the allotted time.

- *Critic:* Tries to get the group to consider alternative possibilities.

- *Facilitator:* Ensures that all members are participating in the group activities, praises individual members for their accomplishments, smooths difficulties, and in general tries to get the group to work together harmoniously.

- *Recorder:* Keeps track of all group decisions and edits the group report.

- *Presenter:* Summarizes the key points of the group report and presents them to the entire class.

- *Checker:* Ensures that all members of the group understand all the points discussed by the group—to this end, may ask individual group members to explain or summarize the material.

- *Elaborator:* Gets the group to relate concepts discussed by the group to material presented earlier in the textbook and in class.

- *Observer:* Monitors how well the group is working together, works for greater cooperation between group members.

Time limits are necessary for in-class group assignments. If some groups have completed the assignment and are waiting for other groups to finish, then the energy developed in the group activity is rapidly dissipated. As noted in Chapter 3, research indicates that students do not concentrate very long during a class if the instructor uses straight lecturing. After little more than 20 minutes, many students have ceased to engage with the lecture. Launching into small-group exercises is a good way to break up the lecture. If handled well, all students and the instructor are energized for the return to the lecture. If the class is large, students will still become bored if all the groups report, so only two groups are asked to present. Then the class as a whole can provide additional comments.

I find that small-group activities are useful in science courses for specific pedagogical purposes. In addition to breaking up the lecture as just discussed, such activities help students to identify misconceptions that they may hold. Small groups can be used as an out-of-class activity that enhances students' critical thinking capacities. One such activity is based on exposing students to philosophers of science. I have used this activity in many courses: a large introductory class on optics and modern physics, an upper-year course in special activity, and a special course given to students in all science disciplines who are members of a particular unit of the university specializing in interdisciplinary research by high-achieving undergraduate students.

Dealing With Dysfunctional Groups

Despite these positive aspects, there may be some students who do not like working in groups. This may be due to less-than-satisfactory prior experiences, personal study habits, or lack of understanding of the benefits of working in small groups.

The first reason leads to an inquiry into the occasional failure of a small group. Sometimes there are problems in the dynamics of the interaction of members of a particular group. Such a problem must be detected early on, otherwise the group may fail to meet its objectives, and the group members will develop a dislike for small-group activities. One way of detecting problems is to have students regularly evaluate the group. If there are serious problems within a particular group, it is essential that you meet with the group as soon as possible. (Make sure, however, that this is not just a temporary problem related to the storming stage in the natural growth of groups.) Indicate to the group members that you have observed a problem, but you are unsure what it is. Listen to what all the group members have to say, then try to get the group to find its own solution to the problem.

Summary

Benefits of Group Activities

- *The small-group format removes some of the impersonality of the large-lecture format, especially for students who are new to the university.*

- *Provides opportunities to develop social interaction skills, network, develop friendships.*

- *Appeals to students with differing learning styles.*

- *Results in better student performance.*

Characteristics of Effective Groups

- *Contain students of differing abilities.*

- *Ideally are four or five students.*

- *Each team member has a well-defined role.*

- *There is some form of individual accountability.*

Dealing With Dysfunctional Groups

- *Detect the problem as soon as possible by using regular evaluations.*

- *Meet with the group.*

- *Listen to all group members.*

- *Try and get the group to find its own solution.*

6

Selected Methods for Using Collaborative Groups

This chapter illustrates how the collaborative group approach can be used in or out of class to produce a *conceptual conflict*, promote more learning by means of *jigsaws*, have students learn in pairs (the *learning cell*), and clarify the understanding of concepts found in the textbook or delivered in the lecture using *cooperative concept mapping*.

Conceptual Conflict

As noted in Chapter 4, students enter science courses with misconceptions. Conceptual change models that attempt to address altering students' conceptions fall into two primary groups. One group consists of those models based on the conceptual conflict model developed by Strike and Posner (1985, 1992), who assert that the more fruitful explanation will be adopted through reason. The other group takes a more structural approach, believing that there is an underlying framework of misconceptions that need to be addressed. Within these two models are 1) Vosniadou's "framework theories" (e.g., Vosniadou & Brewer, 1987), 2) diSessa's "causal net" (diSessa & Sherin, 1998), and 3) Chi's "ontological beliefs" (Chi, Slotta, & deLeeuw. 1994). Several other learning frameworks for conceptual change are given in Duschl and Gitomer (1991). The problem with the structuralist approach is that students coming into the course are not likely to have a coherent, well-defined knowledge of the world, as discussed in Chapter 4.

Hewson and Hewson (1984) discuss changing students concep-tual frameworks by means of conceptual conflict. As they point out, the idea that learning can occur if students are a party to a con-flict of ideas goes all the way back to Dewey (1910) and has been elaborated on by many other authorities since. In particular, Piaget (1977) proposed that disequilibrium, dissatisfaction, or discord must be created within the student between his or her initial con-ception and the to-be-learned one. The attempt to resolve this cog-nitive conflict results in the processes of *assimilation* or *accommodation* of the new idea, as discussed in Chapter 4. This no-tion of dissatisfaction is at the base of several early models of con-ceptual change.

Collaborative groups can be designed in such a way that con-ceptual conflict is produced within the class. However, the condi-tions under which a student can undergo conceptual change need to be identified first. Pintrich, Marx, and Boyle (1993) state that the modern theory of conceptual change assumes that bringing about changes in an individual student is analogous to the nature of change in scientific paradigms proposed by philosophers of sci-ence, particularly Kuhn (1970) and Lakatos (1970). A good discus-sion of this idea is found in Duschl and Gitomer (1991). With these theoretical underpinnings, conceptual change models have become the norm for research on learning in physical and social science and mathematics.

Posner et al. (1982, p. 212) present the idea of conceptual change in the form of two questions:

1) Under what conditions does one central concept come to be replaced by another?

2) What are the features of a conceptual ecology which govern the selection of new concepts?

They answer that

1) Students must know of problems with their per-sonal (alternative) scientific conceptions.

2) The replacement (current textbook) concept must be intelligible. Students must be able to understand how to apply the replacement conception to qualita-tive and quantitative problems presented to them.

3) The replacement concept must be plausible. It must be possible for the student to use the replacement concept to solve all problems that were previously understood in terms of the previously held personal concept.

4) There should be some advantages to using the re-placement concept. This could, for example, be a wider applicability of the new concept. (Posner et al., 1982, p. 212)

Based on this framework, even if the last three features of changing students' concepts occur, students will cling to their per-sonal concepts if they do not identify problems with their personal scientific conception. This occurs because these beliefs make sense in explaining observations students have made about the physical world, and having taken the effort to construct their private under-standing, these same students will not easily relinquish their origi-nal viewpoints.

In my view (Kalman, 1999), students will modify their views if teaching is based on Feyerabend's (1993) principle of counter in-duction: the process by which one scientific theory or idea is used to affect change in its rival. (For a more in-depth discussion of Fey-erabend's analysis, its relationship to conceptual change models, and critical thinking see Kalman, 2002.) Feyerabend notes that evaluation of a theoretical framework doesn't occur until there is an alternative.

A scientist who is interested in maximal empirical content, and who wants to understand as many as-pects of his theory as possible, will adopt a pluralis-tic methodology, he will compare theories with other theories rather than with "experience," "data," or "facts." (Feyerabend, 1993, p. 33)

Halloun and Hestenes (1985a) use the analogy of a balloon to describe students' behavior. Students' assimilation of the replacement concept pushes in the balloon somewhat but leaves their personal concepts fundamentally intact. Sufficient pressure must be applied to actually break the balloon.

Support for this idea is found in an experiment reported in Kalman, Morris, Cottin, and Gordon (1999).

> In September 1997, in a two semester course on physics for non-science students, Dr. Kalman tried the following experiment: The students had read about inertia in the textbook, but only as applied to horizontal motion. Dr. Kalman then presented the sandbag problem to them. By vote the entire class without exception concurred that the sandbag would fall immediately without rising. The correct result, that the sandbag would initially continue with the same speed as the balloon, was then fully explained in terms of inertia. The students expressed themselves as delighted with the correct answer. Dr. Kalman then presented an experiment from the *The Video Encyclopedia of Physics Demonstrations* (Berg, 1992) in which a ball was fired vertically from a "car" moving horizontally at constant velocity. The video asks where the ball will land; in front of, behind or on top of the "car" and then pauses. Fully one half of the class considered that the ball would hit the ground ahead of or behind the "car." (p. S49)

Hewson and Hewson (1984) describe this process as a conceptual conflict. For learning to take place, the student must compare the two conceptions and find them to be in conflict. In the subsequent examination of the two concepts, the student must *not* compartmentalize his or her knowledge. Roth and Lucas (1997) point out that discourse analysis indicates that "people's attitudes—our belief-related talk—(a) depends a great deal on the context; (b) is highly variable within individuals, so that one person often expresses contradictory beliefs (sometimes within a matter of minutes)" (p. 147). Here is where the students' development of critical thinking is essential. Students must realize that two different concepts are presented and subject each to a critical analysis. This is the only way that students will not simply assimilate the replacement concept by compartmentalization of their knowledge. (The balloon is pushed in to make room for the replacement concept but the personal scientific concept is not discarded.)

I use conceptual conflict exercises (Kalman, 1998) to introduce students to the idea that there can be more than one equally logical way of looking at a phenomenon, and only experiment, not logic, can be the determining factor for theory. Students are encouraged to explore different viewpoints on a given phenomenon. An inducement for this exploration is to include an essay question on the midterm and on the final covering the phenomena examined in the conceptual conflict exercises.

Before doing any conceptual conflict exercises, students perform a warm-up exercise in which they introduce themselves to the other group members and then reach a consensus about who were the three greatest scientists of all time. Aside from getting students used to the collaborative group framework, the purpose of this warm-up exercise is for students to practice reaching a joint decision within a fixed time limit. Groups of four to five students are organized to discuss each issue. The students remain in the same group for all exercises.

Overview of the Conceptual Change Experiment

For this experiment, we used four typical personal scientific concepts widely held by students entering an introductory mechanics course. These four were chosen because, in our opinion, they seem to be pivotal in our students' transition from their personal scientific concepts to the Newtonian synthesis. They are:

1) The idea that bodies of different masses falling from rest through a nonviscous medium for a short time (so that the

resistance of the medium can be neglected) are found at later times to move at different speeds.

2) The idea that a fast-moving bullet stays in the air because of its great speed.

3) The idea that if a sandbag is dropped from an ascending balloon, immediately upon release the initial velocity of the sandbag is zero.

4) The idea that a ball thrown in the air is in equilibrium at the highest point in its motion.

As described in Kalman, Morris, Cottin, and Gordon (1999), tests were conducted in fall 1995 and fall 1996 using two sections of the introductory calculus-based mechanics course taught by the same professor. In accordance with the usual procedure in collaborative group exercises, students were asked to take on a particular role within each group. Four students were assigned to a collaborative group. The students remained in the same group for all exercises, but could change roles of reporter, scribe, timekeeper, or critic in each activity. For each exercise, students were presented with a demonstration or qualitative problem and asked to discuss it for a fixed time limit. The time limits were set so that none of the groups had to wait for other groups to complete the task. Typically, all group members became actively involved, often trying mini-experiments with erasers and other objects nearby. The energy of the group activity was carried over to the reporting stage, and often gave the instructor renewed energy. We told the groups that there were at least two ways of looking at the problem, but they must suspend judgment. (For example, until the Coriolis force was understood, one could logically take the position that the earth is at rest or the sun is at rest.) Compartmentalization could occur because students were not clear that there were two distinct conceptual ways of viewing a phenomenon.

The professor toured the classroom while students worked in their groups to find two groups with different explanations of the concept. The two groups chosen reported to the class, thereby setting up a conceptual conflict. Then spokespersons from each group debated the issue between themselves, after which the rest of the students were invited to address questions to this panel of "experts." To highlight that there were two concepts in conflict, the two opposing issues presented by the two groups were clearly stated, and the class then voted on which concept resolved the demonstration or qualitative problem. (Voting is essential because students who have compartmentalized concepts often misinterpret statements in view of their eclectic viewpoint.) Then the professor resolved the conflict by explaining with the aid of experiments how the replacement concept describes the demonstration or qualitative problem in accord with experimental findings, while the personal (alternative) scientific conception fails to do so.

Part of the goal here is for students to clarify their interpretation of nature. Students must be reassured that their current views are reasonable, but there is another viewpoint that is now held to be experimentally correct. Once the differing views of nature are clearly established, the role of experiment in deciding the issue can be emphasized. It is made clear that science is an experimental subject, and the ultimate determination of how things actually work must be an appeal to experiment.

In the initial year of the experiment, attempts were made to produce conceptual change for all four of the Newtonian concepts. Standard statistical tests showed a clear gain for the group experiencing collaborative learning over the control group. Because the same professor taught both sections in the same semester, the results should have given a clear indication of whether our approach was effective. However, the professor teaching the sections, who was used to lecturing supplemented by demonstrations and audio-visual aids, was dubious of the results. He suggested that to be absolutely certain, in the second year a further modified experiment be made. This time in section A, concept 2 of a bullet compared to a dropped penny and concept 3 of a sandbag dropped from an ascending balloon were treated by the collaborative group method and concept 1 comparing the fall of a sheet of paper with a set of keys and concept 4 examining the forces acting on a thrown baseball were treated conventionally. In section B, the procedure was reversed—concepts 1 and 4 were treated by the collaborative group method and concepts 2 and 3 were treated conventionally. Standard statistical tests showed a gain for the group experiencing collaborative learning over the control group in every case. Task sheets for these experiments are found in Appendixes 6.1, 6.2, 6.3, and 6.4.

Jigsaw

The original jigsaw method was developed by Aronson, Blaney, Stephan, Sikes, and Snapp (1978). In its original form, each student receives only part of the learning materials, but is responsible for learning the material given to the other group members as well. Each student learns his or her portion and then must teach it to the other group members. The total material to be learned must be divided into roughly equal amounts. If the team members have equal abilities, it can be divided randomly, or the team members themselves can choose which parts they want to study and teach the others. To help the students become expert in understanding the material, students from all groups in the class who are working on the *same* material might get together as subgroups. Students in these secondary groups help each other understand the material and discuss how they can teach the material to their primary group members.

In the approach that I use, the class is purposely divided into groups. Each group is assigned an entire book to read with the task of viewing course material through the eyes of a modern philosopher of science. Each group of students studies the work of one philosopher of science such as Kuhn (1970), Lakatos (1970), Feyerabend (1993), or Popper (1963) throughout the course. Depending on the course, either 60 minutes a week, or 60 minutes every second week, or five 75-minute sessions are devoted to group presentations. The groups report periodically to the entire class.

The following are the course objectives found in the course outline that all students receive:

Studying different philosophers of science serves several purposes:

1) To understand how science functions. To this end, students examine how some 20th-century philosophers of science understand the scientific process and how theories evolve.

2) To develop the critical thinking skills needed to analyze ideas critically and compare them with observations of how nature functions. Students need to distinguish between concepts, hypotheses, and observations of nature.

For students to grasp the material, they must develop their critical thinking skills. They must come to understand and critically analyze their own views. Only then can they examine the evolution of science and develop ideas about how science works. The students present these ideas to the class and additionally hand in a written version. Only the written version is marked.

The presentations follow the development of certain ideas over a period of time. For the first presentation, the instructions to the students are: "Introduce your group's philosopher and explain his epistemology and methodology." For the remaining group presentations, students are asked to explain how certain scientific developments would be viewed by their philosopher. For each session, only one group studying each philosopher makes a 10-minute presentation. Other groups are asked to comment on the presentation, then the subject is opened to general discussion. Throughout the presentations, the professor suggests further topics for exploration in the next presentations. For example: What is Popper's attitude to verisimilitude? To further enhance the learning of each philosopher's approach, a copy of one (excellent) group report is made available for copying by all students.

In an introductory calculus-based course on optics and modern physics for science students, the changing attitudes toward light are explored. The topics are presented to the students as follows:

1) Discuss the wave and particle theories of light from the point of view of your philosopher. (You might not find these views in a book—it is a problem for you to solve!) In particular, comment on the role of Young's experiment as a *crucial* experiment.

2) Discuss the ether theory (pre-1880) from the point of view of your philosopher.

3) Discuss the Michelson-Morley experiment from the point of view of your philosopher.

4) Discuss the existence of photons from the point of view of your philosopher.

The pedagogical objectives in having students solve these questions are discussed next. The questions are all intended as problems to be solved by the students as noted in the parenthetical remark found in the first question. Many students, nonetheless, seek to find information through books or through the web. Students are supposed to dissect the concepts and experiments. For example, for the second question, they might answer:

1) Bradley in 1727–1728 performed an experiment based on the earth moving with respect to an absolute reference frame (the Ether) in which light moves that seemed to confirm the existence of the ether.

2) Arago wrote a letter in 1810 to Fresnel concerning an experiment that he had made that yielded a result contradicting the simple ether theory.

3) Fresnel modified the ether theory and made a prediction.

4) Fizeau in 1851 executed a beautifully designed experiment (worthy of a Nobel prize if they had been given at the time) that confirmed Fresnel's prediction.

In their written assignment of several pages, students need to be clear about these experiments and theories and the concepts and methodology involved in their design. Then they must examine them from the point of view of their philosopher. How do these experiments and theories fit with their philosopher's views on the progress of science? Does their philosopher consider these experiments and theories to be good science? This leads them to a deeper understanding of the concepts. Student problems with doing the assignment are:

1) As noted previously, they may try and find information from books and/or the web and include the information as the bulk of the answer.

2) They may not clearly set out the theories and experiments.

3) They may put in too much detail on the experiments and theories—particularly details found in their textbook.

4) They may not clearly relate the theories and experiments to their philosopher's views on science.

5) They may not consider (from their philosopher's point of view) whether these experiments and theories are "good science."

A major issue that is discussed by means of student presentation of these assignments is what constitutes a "good" scientific theory. Matthews (1994) notes that the debate of empiricism versus realism "has so dominated the history of philosophical reflection on the nature of science that it ought to feature in school discussions about the nature of science" (p. 177). This is an issue that Matthews ascribes to the liberal tradition.

> The liberal tradition maintains that science education should not just be on education or training *in* science. . . . They [students] should have a feeling for methodological issues, such as how scientific theories are evaluated and how competing theories are appraised. (Matthews, 1994, pp. 2–3)

First and foremost, students learn that there are different views according to the different philosophers as to the answer to each question. Students become aware that the same textual material can be viewed in a variety of ways. Almost all students come to realize that older "replaced" theories were not necessarily "bad" and that presently accepted theories may very well change

On the final examination, students are required to examine a scientific theory that they have never seen before from the point of view of all the philosophers studied in the course. Almost all students are able to answer the question at a satisfactory level. This provides evidence that students have met another of the major goals of the course: the ability to analyze textual material from different points of view.

The Learning Cell

Using pairs to learn new materials is the oldest known use of collaborative groups. Using a pair collaborative group in a form called the "learning cell" is investigated in the university context by Goldschmid and Shore (1974). Many of the points discussed in this section are also found in Schermerhorn, Goldschmid, and Shore (1975), which addresses the same procedure in pre-university education. Goldschmid and Shore propose using the learning cell to redress some of the difficulties associated with learning in large university classes. They point out that small recitation classes as adjuncts to the large lecture are often unsuccessful because, for example, students arrive unprepared for group meetings.

The learning cell is a peer teaching model in which students switch teacher and learner models within the same learning context. Students prepare for the learning cell by reading an assignment and noting questions related to the assigned text. These questions could relate to important concepts found in the reading or problems to be solved. Questions could also deal with other material that relates to the current assignment. For each assignment, students are randomly assigned a partner. They meet and alternate asking questions. The questioner in every case elaborates on or corrects the answer. A variation is basically a jigsaw for two, where each student is assigned different material. Students alternate in teaching their materials to their partner and following up by asking their partners prepared questions.

Goldschmid and Shore (1974) conducted an experiment on 180 students in nine classes in six courses. It was concluded that "students performed significantly better on portions of the class taught by the learning cell." General use of this method indicates that it works best if it is used occasionally, rather than for every class.

Collaborative Concept Mapping

Collaborative concept mapping is a variation of a procedure called concept mapping that began to be studied in detail in the late 1980s (see, for example, Heinze-Fry, 1987, and Cliburn, 1990). Dedic,

Rosenfield, d'Apollonia, and De Simone (1994) combine this strategy with collaborative learning, assuming that when students interact in a collaborative group setting they will be more efficient in deriving meaningful concept maps.

Concept Mapping

A concept map is a visual representation of the relationship between concepts. Students first have to identify important concepts and then show the relationship between them. Concepts are placed in boxes or circles and the relationships are indicated by arrows drawn between them. Often arrows are used to indicate which concepts follow from others. Normally the most general concepts are at the top of the map and specific related concepts are arranged underneath, yielding a hierarchical structure.

Wallace and Mintzes (1990) have shown how concept maps can be used for documenting and exploring concept change in biology. They studied 91 elementary education majors enrolled in five sections of a science education methods course. Six sessions were given as part of successive 75-minute class sessions over a period of three weeks that covered training, practice, review, pretesting, instruction, and posttesting.

In the first session, students were trained in the concept mapping procedure. Hierarchical concept maps and the general terms involved in the construction of the maps, such as concepts, principles, and theories, were introduced. A criterion for marking the concept maps was explained; students were shown examples of student-constructed maps and how they were scored.

In the second session, students were given an opportunity to make their own concept maps. Instructors reviewed the subject and discussed student-generated maps. A homework assignment was given to produce a map based on some textual material.

In the third session, the marked maps were returned, and the method was discussed and reviewed by the class.

In the fourth session, students were given a pretest on "Life Zones in the Ocean." They were then given a set of 10 concept labels on the same topic: life zones in the ocean, abyssal zone, adapt, continental shelf, intertidal zone, mineral, necrotic zone, photosynthetic zone, phytoplankton, and tide. They were asked to construct a concept map using these labels.

In the fifth session, students were randomly assigned to work with a computer-assisted instruction package developed by Prentice-Hall/Edunetics. One package was "Life Zones in the Ocean," consisting of 40 knowledge, comprehensive, and application items, and the other was on "Body Defenses." Although the average time to perform either program is 45 minutes, students were given as much time as they needed and permitted to review portions of the material and take notes.

In the final session, a posttest was administered, and students were again asked to develop a concept map on "Life Zones in the Ocean."

Wallace and Mintzes (1990) conclude, "Concept mapping offers a valid and useful method for looking at changes in cognitive structure" (p. 1045).

Collaborative Concept Mapping

Dedic, Rosenfield, d'Apollonia, and De Simone (1994) describe collaborative concept mapping as an activity that can be integrated into an entire course or used as a stand-alone activity. They suggest familiarizing yourself with this procedure by first trying it as an individual class activity, setting up collaborative groups of three to four students in the manner described in Chapter 5 (establishing interdependence, using icebreakers, etc.). The students could be randomly assigned and asked to set up a concept map of material described in a short text of several hundred words. The following steps are used to implement this procedure:

1) *Integrating concept mapping into the course curriculum.* Within each topic area, select the relevant topics and the concepts that you wish to emphasize. Group these concepts into categories that contain closely related concepts.

2) *Orient students.* Students may have had bad past experiences with group work, may not understand what is required to be in a collaborative group, or may be used to working alone or in

competition with other students. Frank discussions with students about these issues are necessary.

3) *Assign students to groups.*

4) *Knowledge of category.* At least a superficial knowledge of the basic details and terminology used in each category is required.

5) *Instruction on concept mapping.* Never forget that concept mapping is a complex procedure. Students will require a session where the development of a concept map is modeled; that is, a concept map is constructed by the class and the instructor. This class would include asking rhetorical questions, providing partial answers, and summarizing.

6) *Identifying main ideas (individual).* Students are given a particular section of text covering a selected category and asked to identify key concepts. Reflective writing on the text would help. Highlighting, underlining, and listing are possible modes that could be used. This step provides some individual accountability.

7) *Identifying main ideas (group).* Students meet in their groups to review and summarize the content in the assigned material. They then can compare their lists of concepts and prune them into closely related ideas. They also should try and arrange the final list into groups, naming each group by a global concept. This step enhances the interdependence of the group.

8) *Drafting concept map (individual).* Students prepare a draft concept map based on the material identified in Steps 6 and 7. Note the selected material should have been short enough in length so that the concept map will have about 10 to 15 nodes, organized into four or five clusters. It is important in the next step that the various students in the group have somewhat different concept maps. The selected material must be complex enough to ensure that this happens. This step provides some individual accountability.

9) *Revising and using concept maps (group).* Students meet in their groups and compare their individual maps. Individual student understanding of the assigned material should be enhanced as

students explain their maps to each other. Each group must agree on a group concept map to be submitted for credit. This step enhances the interdependence of the group. This group map could be further used in several ways: Groups could be asked to solve problems using the maps. They could integrate them with prior maps to create a concept map of the entire course. A further possibility is to have all the groups exhibit their maps and then have a class discussion on the differences among the maps.

The concept map in Figure 6.1 is an example of a final group concept map given by Dedic et al. (1994) as part of an illustrative example on concept mapping for Mechanics-Work-Energy Theorem in a college physics course.

FIGURE 6.1

Concept Mapping for Mechanics-Work-Energy Theorem

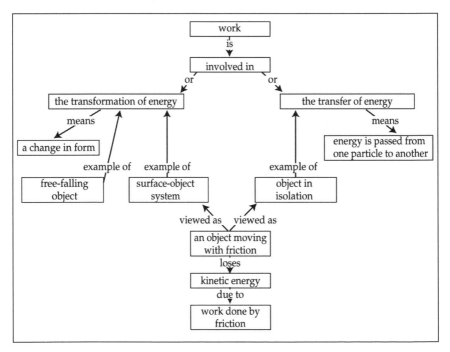

Note. From *Classroom Connections: Understanding and Using Cooperative Learning* by ABRAMI. © 1995. Reprinted with permission of Nelson, a division of Thomson Learning: www.thomsonrights.com. Fax 800-730-2215.

Summary

Conceptual Conflict

- *Students entering gateway science courses are not likely to have a coherent, well-defined knowledge of the world.*

- *Collaborative groups can be designed in such a way that conceptual conflict is produced within the class.*

- *The idea that learning can occur if students are a party to a conflict of ideas goes all the way back to Dewey (1910) and has been elaborated on by many other authorities since.*

Changing Students' Conceptual Frameworks

- *Piaget (1977): Disequilibrium, dissatisfaction, or discord must be created between the student's initial conception and the to-be-learned one.*

- *Based on Feyerabend's (1993) principle of counter induction, it must be made clear to students that there are alternative frameworks. Subsequent analysis creates disequilibrium in the student's mind.*

- *Posner, Strike, Hewson, and Gertzog (1982):*

  1) Students must know of problems with their personal (alternative) scientific conceptions.

  2) The replacement (current textbook) concept must be intelligible. Students must be able to understand how to apply the replacement conception to qualitative and quantitative problems presented to them.

  3) The replacement concept must be plausible. It must be possible for the student to use the replacement concept to solve all problems that were previously understood in terms of the previously held personal concept.

  4) There should be some advantages to using the replacement concept. This could, for example, be a wider applicability of the new concept.

Student Resistance

- *Students will cling to their personal concepts if they do not experience problems with their personal scientific conception.*

- *Halloun and Hestenes (1985a) describe students' personal concepts using the analogy of a balloon.*

- *Students' assimilation of the replacement concept pushes in the balloon somewhat, leaving students' personal concept fundamentally intact. Sufficient pressure must be applied to actually break the balloon.*

- *To break the balloon, students must see that they are being presented with two different concepts and subject the two concepts to critical analysis.*

Conceptual Conflict Exercises Based on Small Groups

- *Students perform a warm-up exercise.*

- *Students remain in the same group for all exercises.*

- *Four students are assigned to a collaborative group. Students remain in the same group for all exercises, but may exchange roles of reporter, scribe, timekeeper, or critic in each activity.*

- *Students are presented with a demonstration or qualitative problem and asked to discuss it for a fixed time limit. The time limits are set so that none of the groups will be waiting for other groups to complete the task.*

- *Two groups with different explanations of the concept are chosen to report to the class.*

- *The spokespersons of each group debate the issue between themselves.*

- *Then the rest of the students are invited to address questions to this panel of "experts."*

- *The two opposing issues presented by the two groups are clearly stated, and the class votes on which concept resolves the demonstration or qualitative problem.*

- *The professor resolves the conflict by explaining with the aid of experiments how the replacement concept describes the demonstration or qualitative problem in accord with experimental findings, while the personal (alternative) scientific conception fails to do so.*

Jigsaw to Relate Philosophers of Science to Course Material

- *Students present their ideas to the class and additionally hand in a written version.*

- *First presentation: Introduce the group's philosopher and explain his epistemology and methodology.*

- *Only one group studying each philosopher makes a 10-minute presentation.*

- *Other groups are asked to comment on the presentation.*

- *Then the subject is opened to general discussion.*

- *The professor suggests further topics for exploration in the next presentations.*

- *A copy of one (excellent) group report is made available for copying by all students.*

- *The presentations follow the development of certain ideas over a period of time.*

The Learning Cell

- *Students prepare by reading an assignment and noting questions. Questions relate to concepts found in the reading or problems to be solved. Questions could also deal with other material that relates to the current assignment. Students are randomly assigned a partner.*

- *Students meet and alternate asking questions.*

- *The questioner in every case elaborates or corrects the answer.*

- *Variation: Each student is assigned different material. Students alternate in teaching their materials to their partner and asking their partner prepared questions.*

Concept Mapping

- *A concept map is a visual representation of relationships among concepts.*

- *Concept mapping can be combined with collaborative learning to enhance student learning.*

Appendix 6.1
Task Sheet A

Part I

1) Form a group with four others who have the same group symbols at the bottom of their task sheet.

2) Assign roles to group members: timekeeper, critic, facilitator, recorder, presenter.

3) Take five minutes to learn about the background of the other group members.

4) Your group has five minutes to produce a list of the three most influential scientists that the world has ever known.

5) Groups will be asked to report on their findings.

Part II

6) Consider the paper and the keys in both experiments. Your group has 10 minutes to produce a transparency describing the following:

   a) What is involved in the motion in each case?

   b) Why do the keys and paper react differently in the first experiment?

   c) What conclusions do you draw from the second experiment?

7) Two groups will report on their findings.

✂ or ☎ or ☞ or ✳ or ✈

APPENDIX 6.2

Task Sheet B

Part I

1) Form in the same groups as in the last class. If you were not present when we formed groups, please come to the front.

2) Groups will discuss each topic for 10 minutes.

3) Each group member is either timekeeper, critic, facilitator, recorder, presenter.

4) Two groups will report to the class. The two presenters from the two groups will remain at the front to discuss viewpoints—first with each other, then with the class. The instructor will moderate the discussion.

5) Afterwards, the instructor will clarify the "correct" situation from an experimental point of view.

Part II

(Put solutions on the supplied transparency. Hand in transparencies and markers at the end of class.)

6) A bullet is fired horizontally from one end of a 10m-long auditorium at 140 m/s.

   a) Describe the motion of the bullet.

   b) Compare its vertical motion with the motion of a penny dropped from the same height at the same time.

APPENDIX 6.3

Task Sheet C

Part I

1) Form a group with four others who have different group symbols at the bottom of their task sheet.

2) Assign roles to group members: timekeeper, critic, facilitator, recorder, presenter.

3) Take five minutes to learn about the background of the other group members.

4) Your group has five minutes to produce a list of the three most influential scientists that the world has ever known.

5) Groups will be asked to report on their findings.

Part II

6) Consider a balloon traveling upwards at 8 m/s. A passenger drops a sandbag over the side of the balloon. Your group has 10 minutes to produce a transparency describing the motion of the sandbag. (Use diagrams and words.)

7) Two groups will report on their findings.

✂ or ☎ or ☞ or ✳ or ✈

APPENDIX 6.4

Task Sheet D

Part I

1) Form in the same groups as in the last class. If you were not present when we formed groups, please come to the front.

2) Groups will discuss each topic for 10 minutes.

3) Each group member is either timekeeper, critic, facilitator, recorder, or presenter.

4) Two groups will report to the class. The two presenters from the two groups will remain at the front to discuss viewpoints— first with each other, then with the class. The instructor will moderate the discussion.

5) Afterwards, the instructor will clarify the "correct" situation from an experimental point of view.

Part II

(Put solutions on the supplied transparency. Hand in transparencies and markers at the end of class.)

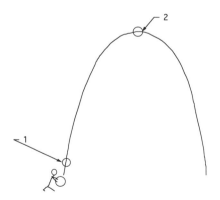

6) What forces act on a thrown baseball?

   a) Just after it leaves your hand

   b) At the top of its motion

7

Changing Students' Epistemologies

Feyerabend (1993) notes that evaluation of a theoretical framework doesn't occur until there is an alternative (principle of counter induction.) In the past, efforts to produce conceptual change among students taking high school science courses and university gateway courses were based on the idea of changing students' theoretical frameworks. As Pintrich, Marx, and Boyle (1993) point out, the modern theory of conceptual change assumes that bringing about changes in an individual student is analogous to the manner in which change occurs in scientific paradigms. These theories are usually based on the descriptions of changes in scientific paradigms proposed by philosophers of science, particularly Kuhn (1970, 1996) and Lakatos (1970).

A major stumbling block in such an effort is that students do not conceive of a subject in terms of a coherent theoretical framework. The student's paradigm in the Kuhnian (1970, 1996) sense is that the subject consists of solving problems using a tool kit of assorted practices (Huffman & Heller, 1995). That is, they do not conceive of the course content in terms of a theoretical framework. Attempts to produce conceptual change by collaborative group exercises or using conceptual concept maps may not be sufficient to get students to change their views on science. Developing a scientific mindset thus may not simply be a conceptual change from personal scientific concepts to scientifically accepted concepts.

Additional factors also led me to believe that more interventions than conceptual conflict exercises and/or conceptual concept maps are needed to make a successful gateway course. Let us keep in mind, as Sternberg (1990) points out, that "in most discourse communities, which are imbued with social traditions, great emphasis is given to such factors as deference to authority, unreflective intuition, social dexterity and timely action" (qtd. in Nelson, 1994, p. 47). One consequence is that it is likely that many students are still playing the "what does the teacher want" game. And as Nelson states in reference to the use of collaborative groups in a course, "students are so resistant to uncertainty that they may suspect a teacher's competence if they are shown two ways of working a problem. . . . When students see that there is no guaranteed right answer in an area, their typical response is that all opinions in the area are equally valid" (p. 52). We must adjudicate various combinations in different contexts. Thinking becomes more complex, we come to see knowledge as constructed rather than discovered. For collaborative learning to be most effective, it is not sufficient simply to have students work together. "Left alone, they often simply create a collage of opinions" (Nelson, 1994, p. 54).

Nelson (1994) suggests that there are three ways of providing students with an intellectual scaffolding that will help students to critically examine the alternatives as models or frameworks that allow students to think about their thinking; as alternative possibilities within disciplinary discourse; or as an introduction to uncertainty, with alternatives to be compared and criteria for comparing them.

I view the conceptual conflict exercises presented in Chapter 6 as the first step in changing student epistemologies. A colleague, Marjorie M. MacKinnon, suggested that I use votes to make clear to students that more than one viewpoint is being discussed. In the sense of Nelson's remarks, many students so resist change that they do not realize that the two groups making presentations are really proposing different points of view. There is also an additional problem. Men's friendships tend to relate to common activities, so men often do not view different perspectives as threatening.

Indeed, I must ensure that the men act in a collegial manner and do not try to stake out territory. Women tend to have friendships based on a commonality of views, and they try to find common points to agree on in a colleague's utterances, rather than seeing an entirely different perspective. When I have two presenters from two groups with diametrically opposing viewpoints, I have often seen a woman presenter try and claim that her colleague from the other group really has the same perspective. Concluding each group activity with a vote on the different views that have emerged helps, but it is not sufficient for many students.

An additional activity—a written *critique*—was introduced to examine alternative possibilities critically. In my course, the critique exercises are worth 5% of the course mark. The critiques are designed to cause students to undergo a *"critical discussion* to decide which natural interpretations can be kept and which must be replaced" (Feyerabend, 1993, p. 59). In the critiques, students are required to present arguments in favor of both their personal scientific concepts and the scientific explanation described by the instructor, with the aid of supporting experiments at the end of the conceptual conflict activity. They must also clearly indicate which position is verified by experimental evidence (with references to the evidence.) Based on these position statements, I find that at most 5% of students still insist that their personal scientific concept is correct. These students are asked to see me.

The reason for doing the critiques is not just to ensure that students are clear on the concept—they might still compartmentalize their views. As we shall see, it is part of an effort to make sure that all students are at Piaget's formal level of intellectual development (see the discussion of Piaget in Chapter 4). We will also see how the activities can fit into a plan to help students identify connections between the various concepts in the course.

In Chapter 6, I described the experiment by Kalman, Morris, Cottin, and Gordon (1999) on a collaborative conflict exercise without the critique component. A conceptual conflict is set up by having two groups with different concepts report to the class. The spokespersons of each group debate the issue between themselves, and then the rest of the students are invited to ask questions of the "experts." Although the results of the Kalman et al. study are statistically impressive, the final posttest scores were low enough in the last three collaborative group conflict exercises that there was room for further improvement.

In winter 1998 and winter 1999, the first of the exercises discussed in Chapter 6 was dealt with using a reflective write-pair-share method, while the three remaining concepts were all considered using conceptual conflict collaborative group exercises. In the Kalman et al. (1999). study, the pretest score on the first exercise was already very high, and thus it was felt that the reflective write-pair-share method would suffice to cover the concept dealt with in that exercise. In 1998, only the collaborative group exercises were used. In 1999, the critique activity was added.

Analysis was done only on those students who wrote both the pre- and posttest and were present at all three conceptual conflict exercises for the winter 1998 and winter 1999 experiments and additionally, only those students who wrote all three critiques for the winter 1999 experiment. The results show a statistically significant improvement in winter 1999 compared with winter 1998 (Kalman, Rohar, & Wells, 2004). In addition to these gains in the two tested concepts for the winter 1999 group over the winter 1998 group, the winter 1999 students also scored better in the baseline consisting of questions that do not relate to the concepts under study. Such a spillover indicates that in doing the critiques, students are not only more likely to undergo conceptual change, but also to increase their critical thinking skills. With such an improvement, students were led to reevaluate their entire conceptual framework.

Students in the 1999 experiment were required to participate in several different activities. In addition to the pre- and posttests, volunteer students were interviewed. Although only a small number of students were intensively interviewed, the students were carefully chosen so that they would be representative. The finding is that through the use of multiple activities, students can become interested in examining the conceptual underpinnings of a course. Table 7.1 shows these students' views on reflective writing, the collaborative group conflict exercises, and writing the critiques based on their interviews. Note that the different activities are ranked differently by different students.

TABLE 7.1

Student Ranking of Activities

Student	Reflective Writing (RW) Ranking of Activity—Comments	Groups (SGW) Ranking of Activity—Comments	Critique (CTQ) Ranking of Activity—Comments
Nabilla	*RW ranked highest of all activities.* • Beginning of course strongly disliked, "was freaking out." • "Write what you think about the new concept, and how does it make sense to you, what you understand, and discussing it with yourself . . . how you think about it, if it makes sense."	*SGW ranked second.* • No change. Final interview: "You start thinking which one makes more sense and which one's logical"	*CTQ ranked last.* • First interview: "Sometimes even questions that you asked to yourself you can find in the critique."
Ahmad	*RW ranked last of all activities.* Originally liked it—RW is "to solidify your ideas about what you read." • Later dislikes. Final interview: "I don't put in a real effort . . . I just want to get . . . a good mark."	*SGW ranked highest.* • No change. Final interview: "The group work gives you new ideas and helps you solidify your opinion about it."	*CTQ ranked second.* • "SGW bombards you with many ideas. . . . CTQ you're going in the opposite direction, you're trying to get rid of all the ideas and come to one right idea."
Solomon	*RW ranked highest of all activities.* • No change. Final Interview: "When you're reflective writing, you're thinking about the concepts and it makes you work through them."	*SGW ranked last.* No change. Final Interview: "I don't think it was helpful"	*CTQ ranked second.* • No change. Final interview: "I don't find it particularly helpful because I don't feel at the end there's a conclusion that is necessarily drawn out."
Alexis	*RW ranked highest of all activities.* • Final interview: "At the beginning the way I thought about it, and the way I think about it now, is way different." • First interview: "Because I have to write I will have to think about it . . . see what you understand about it or what you don't understand."	*SGW ranked last.* • No change. "The problems were too trivial in SGW."	*CTQ ranked highest.* • No change. Final interview: "Always interesting problems. You had to examine why it was so, examine why others saw it in a different way."
Lelana	*RW ranked last of all activities.* • No change. First interview: "I hate writing English essays. . . . And the fact that I have to do it in physics—its just a pain. . . . To actually sit down and learn, I have to read every single line and take notes as I am reading it."	*SGW ranked second.* • Final interview: "It was a good experience, critiques helped, and small groups as well. . . . It was different from the physics classes I had before . . . in the other ones, the teacher just writes a bunch of formulas and it's like memorize these. It was a good change."	*CTQ ranked first.* • Final interview: "The critique was most helpful. This is because the stuff we discussed. . . . I never knew much about them. . . . It (the answers) did not directly come from the book. I had to discuss with this and that person. It came from what I thought...my own thoughts like from my understanding, from my point of view."

Constructing an Epistemology

Students may only initially have a loosely organized, compartmentalized set of concepts. If an activity like collaborative concept maps discussed in Chapter 6 is used, such students are likely to view the various concept maps produced on the different parts of the course as loosely connected, like pearls on a string. This section describes how I work around this problem in the first gateway course that students encounter in the physics sequence.

In order to get students to take a holistic view of the concepts and relate them together, they are presented with two alternative frameworks: pre-Galilean physics and Newtonian physics. The course is designed so that students initially view the frameworks in a theatrical sense—as a drama involving a conflict of actors: Aristotle, Galileo, Newton, and others. As participants passing through a series of interventions, the students become aware that the frameworks relate concepts from different parts of the course and learn to evaluate the two alternative frameworks. They develop a scientific mindset, changing their outlook on the course material from the viewpoint that it consists of a tool kit of assorted practices, classified according to problem type, to the viewpoint that it comprises a connected structure of concepts.

Students' exploration of the concepts in the course occurs through five different activities as shown in Table 7.2. As noted in the timeline, the course includes four components, each of which contains activities found in the previous section or earlier chapters and ranked by the students in Table 7.1.

The course (mechanics) is the first one-semester course in a sequence of three courses covering an introduction to physics. Typically, there are approximately 100 students in each section. The student population in the course is multicultural and multilingual and ranges from freshman to graduate students. Students in this course include science majors, humanities majors, and engineers. At my university, there are usually many foreign students, including at least 20% from Middle Eastern countries. Additionally, a significant portion of the students are returning to school, often after having completed a degree in another discipline.

TABLE 7.2

Timeline for Course Events

Component 1	Component 2	Component 3	Component 4
Reflective Writing	*Reflective Write-Pair-Share* Week 1: $v = 0$ does not imply that a body is stopped Week 2: $a = 0$ does not imply that a body has constant velocity Week 3: Clash of Aristotelian and Galilean viewpoints on the rate of fall of bodies in a vacuum		
Reflective Writing	*Concept Conflict Exercise* Week 4: Independence of horizontal and vertical motion Week 5: Inertia Week 7: Forces acting on a ball thrown in the air	*Critique* Week 5: Independence of horizontal and vertical motion Week 7: Inertia Week 9: Forces acting on a ball thrown in the air	*Midterm* Week 5: Essay on topics discussed in the write-pair-share and/or critique *Final* After week 13: Essay question on critiques from week 7 and/or week 9

Reflective Writing

The reflective writing activity is "workshopped" in class. Students are asked to try understanding the material, though they are cautioned not to expect to understand everything. One reason for the activity is to generate questions in class about what they don't understand. Rivard (1994) points out that writing can be used to enhance the learning of science content and that writing is intimately connected to thinking. Reflective writing engages students with the material before the class even meets (Kalman & Kalman, 1997). Its purpose is to allow the learner to relate prior knowledge to new material and to use self-dialogue about recorded ideas to continue the process of comprehension. Students are given a weekly concept assignment based on the compulsory readings for each class. With the exception of the first class, readings are to be done before class. During the class, it is assumed that students have read the assigned material. Some of the material and problems found in these readings are not covered in class, but students are told that the exam is based on everything found in the readings.

Reflective Write-Pair-Share: Weeks 2 and 3

The first two reflective write-pair-share activities explore displacement, instantaneous velocity, and acceleration (Kalman, 1999, 2002). Students are to see that $v = 0$ at one particular time does not imply that the body is stopped and $a = 0$ at one particular time does not imply that a body has constant velocity.

The third intervention contrasts Galileo's views with that of Aristotle about bodies falling near the earth's surface in a vacuum. It is noted that Aristotle is against idealizations. Since a vacuum doesn't exist, the speed of a body in a vacuum should not be considered. This is contrasted with Galileo's viewpoint that it is useful to consider idealizations of phenomena occurring in the real world.

Conceptual Conflict Exercise: Weeks 4, 5, and 7

Through the conceptual conflict exercise, students are introduced to the idea that there can be more than one equally logical way of looking at a phenomenon, and that only experiment, not logic, can decide the issue. During the intervention, many students realize that other students in the class hold different viewpoints about motion. Students are encouraged to explore this point. An inducement for this exploration is that there are essay questions on the sample midterm and sample final. Students are notified that their midterm and final will be very similar to the sample midterm and final. At the end of the collaborative group exercise, students view experiments from *The Video Encyclopedia of Physics Demonstrations* (Berg, 1992).

Group Work

> In the group work, I asked my friends, so what did you think of it? It wasn't like "Okay, look at chapter five and the answer's right there."
>
> The last few times he [Ahmad] was in my group and we usually end up arguing, because he usually thinks differently than I do. It's good challenging each other.
>
> *—Student interview with Lelana*

The first collaborative group/critique exercise focuses on the independence of horizontal and vertical motion. Students are asked to compare the motion of a dropped object with an object thrown horizontally. It is noted that no information or experiment done up to this point in the course can be used to predict the outcome of this experiment.

The second collaborative group/critique exercise is an examination of a sandbag dropped from a hot air balloon rising at constant speed. Again, it is emphasized that no information or experiment done to date can predict the outcome of this experiment. The professor describes how Galileo used ideal situations to theorize about and eventually derive the law of inertia. The professor explains that Galileo believed that this law is necessary to understand the Copernican perspective.

The final collaborative group/critique exercise continues the discussion of Galileo's revolutionary idea of inertia. Students are asked to examine the forces acting on a thrown baseball just after it leaves the hand and when it reaches the top of its motion. This brings out in the open a variety of students' personal scientific conceptions including "force being dependent on velocity" and the "force of the hand" balancing the force. In summary, the professor emphasizes the concept of equilibrium and the role of inertia in keeping the ball moving.

> [In the final collaborative-group exercise we] had three different opinions and everybody tried to defend his or her own opinion. There was no consensus. We did succeed in identifying those critical points in the problem, why or why not we agree on it, so in this case, I found it very helpful. What really helped was the final explanation by the professor, how it really worked or how that particular situation was supposed to be looked at. It did help in a way that I could point out more precisely the different ways of looking at that particular problem.
>
> —*Student interview with Alexei*

Critique: Weeks 5, 7, and 9

Each of the three conceptual conflict exercises is followed up two weeks later when students hand in a written work, called a *critique,* in which they are required to present arguments in favor of their personal scientific concepts and of the Newtonian explanation. They must clearly indicate which position is verified by experimental evidence with references to the evidence. In correcting the critiques, more than 95% of students now know the "correct" Newtonian position on each phenomenon. Nonetheless, it is essential to have the students state the correct position to correct those few students who do not understand the Newtonian picture. The three critique exercises are found in Appendix 7.1.

> You had to write more than two pages. I had to discuss with this and that person, and it didn't come directly from the book because it wasn't from the book. It came from what I thought. . . . It wasn't com-

ing from a source, so it was from my understanding
and from my point of view.

> *—Student interview with Lelana*

As students progress through the course activities, they reflect
on their belief structures. They eventually see the interrelationship
of the concepts and undergo a change in their mindset.

> In the second critique or third critique, I started
> thinking to a previous critique, so it all builds upon
> itself. The first critique will help explain the second,
> and that helps to explain the third.
>
> *—Student interview with Ahmad*

Assessment

In the midterm and final examinations, everything comes together.
If an atmosphere of trust has been established, students may describe their views in interesting ways, as the following sample illustrates.

> Throughout the ages, people have been fascinated
> by the way things move, and many have postulated
> as to the exact explanations of movement.
>
> Galileo had an inordinate curiosity concerning the
> mechanics of movement. He was forever dropping
> rocks, throwing things at his neighbors, and gener-
> ally being an unmitigated nuisance that he was
> eventually chucked into jail for disturbing the peace
> and insisting on shouting out heretical ideas about
> planets and such.
>
> Aristotle, on the other hand, said some lovely things
> about aesthetics and poetry, and never lobbed
> stones at his friends. He also adhered to the time-
> honored wisdom that the earth was flat. (I don't be-
> lieve he ever went to jail.)
>
> Galileo was in general a rabble-rouser, and much
> more interesting. He let a big stone and a small one

drop from rest off the Leaning Tower of Pisa, and noticed that the two stones hit two people on the head at the same time. From this, he decided that any two objects will fall with constant acceleration. In fact, if one could eliminate air resistance altogether, all objects, despite their shape, would fall at the same rate, due to gravity.

Now, as to the motion of a rock thrown horizontally, one would assume the acceleration would be somehow different. If Galileo threw a rock at his wife, who was a few feet away from the Tower of Pisa, and at the same time dropped a rock onto his dog standing directly beneath him under the tower, one might think that the dog would get hit first.

Not so! The motion of a projectile can be divided into horizontal and vertical components of acceleration, a_x and a_y. While the stone is flying toward his wife, it experiences downward acceleration due to gravity, just the same as the freely falling stone, but no horizontal acceleration, if we neglect air resistance. So, the dog and the wife get nailed at the same time: $a_x = 0$; $a_y = 9.8 \text{ m/s}^2$.

One can also separate the velocity components into v_x and v_y. V_x remains constant because it experiences no acceleration, but v_y will change according to downward acceleration and time. So, $v_x = v_{x,0} =$ constant; $v_y = v_{y,0} = gt$.

What is interesting is that these laws of acceleration and motion only hold true if the body is close to the earth's surface. We can only assume the acceleration due to gravity is constant and downward so long as the range of motion is small compared with the radius of the earth. In fact, we assume that the earth is flat over the range of motion in study. So, one up for Aristotle!

Summary

- *As Pintrich, Marx, and Boyle (1993) point out, the modern theory of conceptual change assumes that bringing about changes in an individual student is analogous to the nature of change in scientific paradigms proposed by philosophers of science. A major stumbling block in such an effort is that students do not conceive of the subject in terms of a coherent theoretical framework. The student's paradigm in the Kuhnian sense is that the subject consists of solving problems using a tool kit of assorted practices. Hence, they do not conceive of the course content in terms of a theoretical framework.*

- *Nelson (1990) notes that "students are so resistant to uncertainty that they may suspect a teacher's competence if they are shown two ways of working a problem." Nelson suggests that there are three methods of intellectual scaffolding that will help students to critically examine the alternatives: "as models or frameworks that allow students to think about their thinking; as alternative possibilities within disciplinary discourse; or as an introduction to uncertainty, with alternatives to be compared and criteria for comparing them."*

- *Conceptual conflict group exercises can be used as the first step in changing student epistemologies. Concluding each group activity with a vote on the different views that have emerged helps, but is not sufficient for many students. An additional activity—a written critique—helps students to examine alternative possibilities critically.*

- *The course is designed so that students initially view the frameworks almost in a theatrical sense—as a drama involving a conflict of actors: Aristotle, Galileo, Newton, and others. Students' exploration of the concepts in the course occurs through five different activities. As participants passing through a series of interventions, the students become aware that the frameworks relate concepts from different parts of the course and learn to evaluate the two alternative frameworks. They develop a scientific mindset that changes their outlook on the course material from the viewpoint that it consists of a tool kit of assorted practices, classified according to problem type, to the viewpoint that it comprises a connected structure of concepts.*

APPENDIX 7.1
Critiques

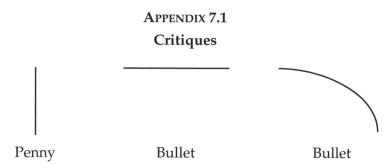

Penny   Bullet   Bullet

On the left is a picture of a penny being dropped. Simultaneously, a bullet is fired. To the center and right are possible pictures of the bullet's motion. Why would some believe that the motion is as depicted in the center and others believe that the motion is as depicted at the right? (Give as many reasons as possible for each viewpoint.)

Critique 1: Suggested length two pages; there is no page limit.

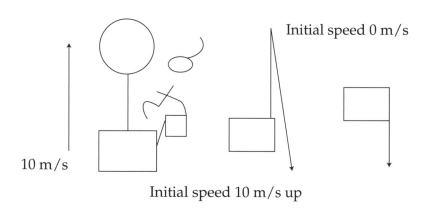

Initial speed 0 m/s

10 m/s

Initial speed 10 m/s up

On the left is a sandbag being dropped from a balloon. (Give as many reasons as possible for reach viewpoint.)

Critique 2: Suggested length two pages; there is no page limit.

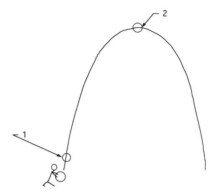

Critique 3: Suggested length two pages; there is no page limit.

8

Problem Solving

This chapter examines why some students have trouble solving problems in science courses and provides some fundamental instruction to use with students to help them solve problems.

Solving Problems Using Templates Versus Solutions Using Paradigms

A colleague once said that if he gave students a problem involving the collision of a Volkswagen Beetle and a cement mixer and then gave them the identical problem on an examination involving the collision of a Mercedes SUV and a Mac truck, most students would not relate the two problems (similar to Gick and Holyoak's story and Duncker's radiation problem described in Chapter 1). According to VanderStoep and Seifert (1994), "Many studies have shown that students often have difficulty abstracting a principle from examples, encoding information into flexible memory representations, and accessing the appropriate principle in new problem contexts" (p. 27).

Until midway through high school, students can be successful at courses by memorizing templates for every situation encountered on an examination. As the number of potential problems that can be presented on tests increases, memorizing becomes more difficult for students to maintain without drastic drops in their marks. The key point is that students lack the ability to apply principles garnered from one problem to an apparently different problem (Gick & Holyoak, 1980, 1983). To meet this change, students must make a shift in their learning from template solving (what Salomon and Perkins, 1989, call *low-road transfer*) to solution by paradigms (what Salomon and Perkins call *high-road transfer*—procedures to apply principles abstracted from many sample problems).

A novice problem solver can be trained to see the connection between Problems 1 and 2 in Figure 8.1 and thus how all problems involving moving objects in air can be solved using a similar set of equations.

FIGURE 8.1

Novice Problem Solver

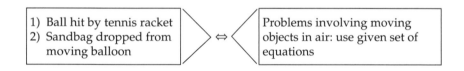

In contrast, an expert can see the connection between Problems 1 and 2 in Figure 8.2 and thus how the exposed moving charge in the power line is analogous to the point source of light. The power line problem is now solved.

FIGURE 8.2

Expert Problem Solver

Problem: Find a point in a power line where the insulation has come off.

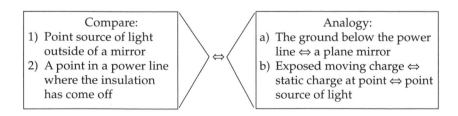

Novice problem solvers look for a template in solving problems—what problem is like the problem they have to solve? "They search for and manipulate equations, plugging numbers into the equations until they have a combination that yields the answers" (Heller, Keith, & Anderson, 1992, p. 628). They do not use conceptual knowledge to analyze the problems, and they don't systematically make plans for solving the problems. "When they arrive at a numerical answer, they are usually satisfied—they rarely check to see if the answer makes sense" (Heller et al., 1992, p. 628). Students can use the following five steps to solve the problems.

Five-Step Method for Solving Problems

Problem-solving ability depends on thinking skills and a knowledge base. But, problem solving performance also depends on a state of mind, as does learning. . . . We do not solve problems because we fear failure. We do not solve problems because we believe that we cannot. The states of mind that lead to such situations are linked to our attitudes as human problem solvers. (Rubinstein & Firstenberg, 1987, p. 24)

1) Translate the problem into a visual representation.

2) Describe the problem—use their qualitative understanding of concepts and principles to represent and examine the problem in science/engineering terms.

3) Plan a solution—translate the elements of the problem into mathematical terms.

4) Execute the plan—find the unknowns and determine how to obtain solutions for them.

5) Examine the solution and see if the values make scientific/engineering sense.

In reading a problem, try to sort out the information that will help you solve the problem ("given" information) from the part to be solved (the "unknown"). In Step 4 of the five-step method, students need to pursue their identification of unknowns to find other equations. Howard McAllister pointed out better ways of problem solving (see www.hawaii.edu/suremath/) and collaborated with me on working out some problems for my students to use. Some of the following problems stem from this collaboration. For Step 4, McAllister tells students to find out what the problem is asking for. The difficulty is that students do not understand how problems in their textbook are constructed. I tell them that the unknowns occurring in Step 4 can be thought of as an embedded problem. For the moment, they should ignore the original problem and solve the embedded problem. Embedded problems may contain further embedded problems so they should keep going until they run out of unknowns.

Problem-Solving Strategies

The remainder of this chapter presents some sample problems.

Problem 1

You are located in a boat equipped with a radar set on a lake. You spot a boat heading in your direction. A pulse emitted from the radar set in your boat is reflected from the oncoming boat and returns in 0.06 μs. How far away is the boat that reflected the pulse?

Solution

- Given 1: "A pulse is emitted from a radar set and returns."
  Draw a diagram to show this.

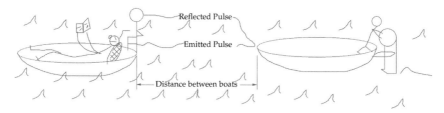

- Given 2: "0.06 μs." Note all numerical information in a list:

  elapsed time, $t = 0.06 \times 10^{-6}$ s $= 6 \times 10^{-8}$ s

- **Unknown 3:** "How far away is the boat that reflected the pulse?" Scan the problem and choose exactly what you are asked to find: distance between the boats as shown in the above figure. Then try and identify this part with equations:

  distance = (speed)(time)

Be careful to ensure that the quantity in the equation matches the unknown. In this case, looking at the diagram, note that the pulse travels the distance between the boats twice (once on emission and the second time on return). The actual distance between the boats is then half the distance traveled by the pulse:

distance (between boats) = ½ (speed of pulse)(elapsed time)

Check which parts of the equation correspond to information on your list (in this case, elapsed time, $t = 0.06 \times 10^{-6}$ s) and which parts are unknown (distance, speed). So far we have an equation involving our given and our unknowns:

$$d = ½ \text{ (speed of pulse)}(6 \times 10^{-8} \text{ s})$$

In order to obtain a value for the distance, we need to have a value for the speed. In general, an additional equation may be needed to find the value of an unknown, such as the speed. In this case, the value of the speed of a radar pulse is the speed of light (3×10^8 m/s). Hence:

distance = ½ $(3 \times 10^8$ m/s$)(6 \times 10^{-8}$ s$) = 9$ m

The problem just solved contains at least one simplification because the speed of the other boat is neglected. Such a simplification is justified only if the distance traveled by the pulse (18 meters) is not noticeably changed by neglecting the speed of the other boat.

Problem 2

Suppose that in Problem 1, the neighboring boat has a speed of 10 m/s as measured from your boat. What effect does this have on the calculation of the distance between the boats?

Solution

The radar pulse traveled 9 m to reach the other boat and an additional 9 m to return to the radar set. When the pulse begins traveling back to the radar set, the boat is moving at 10 m/s. The boat continues to move at this speed of 10 m/s during the return journey of the pulse and so the boat is not exactly 9 m away when the pulse arrives back at the radar set. The exact distance, d, traveled by the boat during the return journey of the pulse is given by:

The elapsed time, t, for the return journey of the pulse is *half* the total time it took for the pulse to go from the radar set to the other boat and return.

$$d = v\,t$$

$$= (10 \text{ m/s})(3 \times 10^{-8} \text{ s})$$

$$= 3 \times 10^{-7} \text{ m}$$

Since this distance is small compared to 9 m, the motion of the neighboring boat was rightfully ignored in Problem 1.

Problem 3

The speed of a particular car is directly proportional to the elapsed time:

$$v \propto t$$

Assuming that the car is moving at 2 m/s at time $t = 1$ second, what is its acceleration at time $t = 2$ seconds?

Solution

1) Discover what you are asked to obtain. This usually appears after words such as *find, show that,* or *what.* In this problem you find the words *what is the acceleration.*

2) What do you know about the variable that you are asked to obtain? In this case the definition:

$$a = \frac{dv}{dt}$$

3) Take the equations obtained in Step 2 one at a time and see what variables are truly unknown; that is, variables whose values are not given numerically in the problem:

The speed v

4) Unknowns obtained in this way generate separate *embedded* problems. Basically we are back to Step 2: What do you know about this variable? For embedded problems, always check the problem statement first. In this case you discover:

a) The *speed* $v \propto t$. Using k for the constant of proportionality,
$$v(t) = kt$$

b) The car is moving at 2 m/s at time $t = 1$ second Since m/s is the unit of speed, this is also a statement about speed, namely
$$v(t) = 2 \text{ m/s, when } t = 2s$$

5) Combining the two statements about the speed yields
$$k(2\text{ s}) = 2\text{ m/s}$$

or

$$k = 2\text{ m/s}^2$$
$$\text{So: } v(t) = 2\,t$$

6) We can now return to the original problem (Step 2):
$$a = \frac{dv}{dt} = 2\text{ m/s}^2 \text{ at all times}$$

Note: In problem solving, you must focus (for a time) only on part of the problem. Pick out of the problem only what you are asked for (Step 1, Step 3), and then *write some equations.*

Problem 4

At the instant the traffic light changes to green, you start your car moving with a constant acceleration of 1.0 m/s². At the same time, a bus traveling at a constant speed of 8.0 m/s overtakes and passes you.

a) How far from your starting point will you overtake the bus?

b) When you overtake the bus, how fast are you traveling?

Solution

Where possible, *always* draw a diagram in solving problems	Begin by drawing a diagram. Taking the x-axis as the direction of motion and the traffic light at $x_{0,car} = x_{0,bus}$
Since the car and the bus start off at the same places at the same time, it is convenient to set $t_0 = 0$. This simplifies the equations. If they had started at different times, then t_0 (at least for one of the vehicles) should not be set to zero.	CAR $\quad$ Start ($t_0=0$) $\qquad\qquad$ Finish ($t_f=t$) $v_{0,car}=0 \qquad a_{car}=1.0m/s^2 \qquad v_{f,car}=v$ $x_{0,car}=0$ $\longleftarrow \quad x \quad \longrightarrow$ BUS $v_{0,bus}=8m/s \qquad a_{bus}=0 \qquad v_{f,bus}=8m/s$ $x_{0,bus}=0$

1) What is asked for? The words *How far from* in Part A imply that you must find the position of the car when it overtakes the bus. Note that $x - x_0 = \Delta x$ is the same for both the car and the bus:

$$x_{car} = x_{bus}$$

2) What do you know about the variable that you are asked to obtain? For constant acceleration problems x is given by

$$v^2 = v_0^2 + 2ax$$

or

$$x = v_0 t + \tfrac{1}{2}at^2$$

3) Take the equations obtained in Step 2 one at a time and see what variables are truly unknown, that is, variables whose values are not given numerically in the problem:

$$\text{CAR: } v_{car}^2 = v_{0,car}^2 + 2ax_{car} \Rightarrow v_{car} = 2(1.0)x_{car}$$
$$\text{BUS: } v_{bus}^2 = v_{0,bus}^2 + 2ax_{bus} \Rightarrow v_{bus} = 8 \text{ m/s}$$

v_{car} and the v_{bus} are different; hence, this pair of equations has no simultaneous solution:

CAR: $x_{car} = v_{o,car}t_{car} + \frac{1}{2} a_{car}t_{car}^2$ (1)

BUS: $x_{bus} = v_{o,bus}t_{bus} + \frac{1}{2} a_{bus}t_{bus}^2$ (2)

4) Take the equations one at a time and see what variables are truly unknown; that is, variables whose values are not given numerically in the problem. We have:

$$x_{car}, x_{bus}, t_{car}, \text{ and } t_{bus}$$

5) What do you know about these variables? Looking at the diagram, it is clear that since your car and the bus are at the same position at the start and again at the finish, x is the same in equations (1) and (2). That is:

$$x_{car} = x_{bus} = x$$
$$\text{Moreover}$$
$$t_{car} = t_{bus} = t$$

Hence we can eliminate x from equations (1) and (2) resulting in

$$\frac{1}{2} t^2 = 8t$$

This is a quadratic equation and has two roots:

$$t(t - 16) = 0; t = 0 \text{ s or } t = 16 \text{ s}$$

Both are physically correct. The equation $t = 0$ s represents the first time the car and the bus are together (the distance x is the same for the car and the bus).

FIGURE 8.3

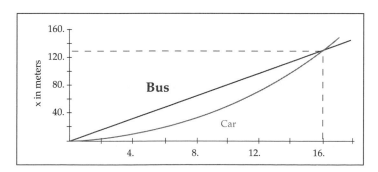

Displacement of the bus and the car at various times. Where the two graphs intersect, the bus and the car have the same displacement; that is, they are side by side. Note the intersection points correspond to the two roots of $\frac{1}{2} t^2 = 8t$; $t = 0, 16$ s.

Similarly $t = 16$ s represents the next time the car and the bus are together (see Figure 8.3). Substituting $t = 16$ s into equation (1) shows that the car has traveled $x = 8(16) = 130$ m. The speed will be

$$v = v_0 + at$$
$$= 0 + 1.0 \ (16) \ \text{(see Figure 8.3)}$$
$$= 16 \ \text{m/s}$$

(How fast is this in the usual units for the speed of the car? Fast enough to get a traffic ticket?)

These four problems are covered in the first few weeks of the course. Many students are very worried about doing problems. Some even suffer from mathematics anxiety. The important thing is to show these students ways to get started doing the problems. I tell students who are troubled that we will work on how to solve problems the entire semester and they need to keep working on the process. Since they passed all the prerequisites for the course, they are *capable* of doing the problems and passing the course.

To help them, I make the midterm a "vocabulary" test. It covers the concepts taught up to the midterm, but only includes simple problems. Students receive a sample midterm and a sample final, and are told that hard problems will only be on the final. To ensure that students can do the difficult problems and to deal with cheating on the assignments, the course outline stipulates that students must pass the final to get a mark of C or higher for the course.

Some students who are in trouble at the time of the midterm do better on the final examination. After handing out the midterm, I give students an incentive. The course outline reads that the final examination and the midterm are each worth 30% of their mark. But for those students who improve their mark on the final examination compared to the midterm, the final will be worth 45% and the midterm 15%. I read the class a letter from a student who actually received 0% on the midterm but passed the final, receiving a respectable mark for the course. His letter is included in Appendix 8.1.

After the first few weeks, try to get students thinking about concepts in a more general fashion. One important step is to introduce another problem that doesn't look like Problem 4, but is solved in the same way as Problem 4, shown in Problem 5.

Problem 5

A man tosses a block of wood straight up into the air, releasing it 1.8 m from the ground at a speed of 25 m/s. 1.8 seconds later, a woman standing on a platform beside the man fires a rifle straight up at the block. If the bullet leaves the gun at a speed of 176 m/s and at a height 3.1 m above the ground, find

a) How long it takes before the bullet hits the block

b) How high above the ground the bullet is when it strikes the block

Solution

First draw a diagram:

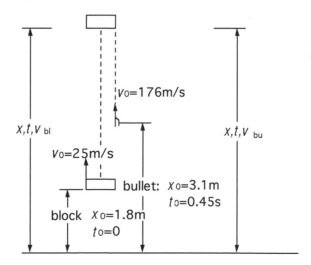

I ask students: *Is this problem like another problem that we have solved recently?* After some discussion, students realize that it is indeed very much like Problem 4. The block and the bullet meet at the same distance above the ground, just as the car and bus move the

same distance from their mutual starting point. In order that the time has the same value when the bullet meets the block, the time is measured from the instant the block leaves the man's hand. Then when the bullet meets the block, the distance from the ground x and the elapsed time t are the same for both the bullet and the block. Only the velocity of the bullet, v_{bu} and the velocity of the block v_{bl} are different. Now what is asked for: the distance x and the elapsed time t. What equations can be used to solve for x and t?

$$x = x_0 + (v_0)(t - t_0) + \tfrac{1}{2}g(t - t_0)^2$$

block $x = 1.8\text{m} + (25\text{ m/s})(t - 0) + \tfrac{1}{2}(-9.8\text{m/s}^S)(t - 0\text{s})^2$
$= 1.8 + (25\text{ m/s})t - (4.9\text{m/s}^2)t^2$ (1)

bullet $x = 3.1\text{ m} + (176\text{ m/s})(t - 1.8\text{s}) + \tfrac{1}{2}(-9.8\text{m/s}^2)(t - 1.8\text{s})^2$
$= -329.6\text{m} + (193.6\text{m/s})t - (4.9\text{m/s}^2)t^2$ (2)

Eliminate x from equations (1), (2) yielding
$$0 = -331.4 + (168.6\text{m/s})t$$
or
$$t = 1.966\text{ s}$$

Since the bullet was fired 1.8 s after the block was tossed into the air, the bullet struck the block 0.17 s after being fired. Substituting t = 1.966 s into either equation (1) or equation (2) shows that the block and the bullet were 32m above the ground when the bullet struck the block.

Summary

- *Novice problem solvers look for a template when solving problems. Until midway through high school, students can be successful at courses by memorizing templates for every situation encountered on an examination. But as the number of potential problems that can be presented on tests increase, this mode becomes more difficult for students to maintain without drastic drops in their marks.*

- *Students lack the ability to apply principles garnered from one type of problem to an apparently different problem. To deal with this per-*

ceived change, students must make a shift in their learning from template solving to solving by paradigms—procedures to apply principles abstracted from many sample problems. They can use a five-step method to help sort out information given and the part to be solved (the unknown).

- Students who are challenged are told they are capable of doing the problems and passing the course. The class receives sample midterm and final exams. Some students do better on the final than on the midterm and so are able to pass the course with a grade of a C or higher.

APPENDIX 8.1
Letter From a Student

To Whom It May Concern:

I am writing this letter in hope that it may benefit or encourage some students who are taking Physics 204 and who at some point feel as though they are struggling to keep their heads above water.

At the beginning of this course I was eager and excited by the opportunity to explore the wonderful world of physics. I had been told that it was a challenging course and would require a great deal of discipline and dedication. Nevertheless, I assumed that my ambitious work ethic and curiosity would somehow pull me through. Unfortunately, what I discovered is that positive motivation can be negatively affected when you are dealing with formulas and theorems that seem to defy the rules of what to the average mind seems logical.

I began to realize just how much trouble I was having in physics when I received the results of my midterm. I had studied hard and felt that I was prepared for this exam. Unfortunately, studying without understanding does not result in anything but frustration. I believed I had understood the information I was going to be tested on. What happened, however, was that I attempted to use logical reasoning instead of theory when solving complex problems. I am not embarrassed to admit that I received a grade of 0% on the midterm. This was not the result of bad study habits or a lack of preparation. It was the result of confusion. Discouraged, but not ready to give up the fight, I decided to approach physics in a different way.

The following information may serve as valuable insight to those of you who may experience the same level of difficulty that I had, and hopefully it will be as beneficial to you as it was for me. My first piece of advice is follow the course outline and complete all class assignments. They serve as constructive reference tools when preparing for exams and clear up any misunderstandings you may have had throughout the course. The critiques are another valuable tool. What I found about doing these assignments was that they helped me to develop a physics mindset. The diagrams allow you to visualize the momentum, direction, velocity, and any other essential components of the objects in question and help in understanding how the application of physics impacts one's surroundings.

By following the above-mentioned advice you may feel as though you are making some ground and quite confident that you have a handle on physics. Whatever you do, do not become overconfident! Some students feel as though they have mastered physics and therefore do not consider going to class as a top priority. Wrong! This is perhaps the worst mistake you could make. Never assume that you know more than the experts. Physics professors are a wealth of information. They may present a lesson in a way that helps make sense of something that previously had you baffled. If you do have some concerns that need to be cleared up, lectures serve as a question-and-answer period. Not only will you have the opportunity to ask questions, but listening to the questions of your fellow classmates may also be extremely beneficial.

At this point I would like to conclude by saying that in addition to completing all in-class assignments and regularly attending class, I had to do a lot of work on my own. Everyone develops his or her own study methods that work best for them. After the midterms I went back and started from square one. I approached the physics textbook chapter by chapter, highlighting key concepts that are essential to the mechanics of physics. I attempted problem after problem, never giving up until I had figured out and completely understood how to arrive at the correct solution. This is a time-consuming and frustrating process; however, it was beneficial in the end. When I had completed my review I went back and attempted problems that we had worked on in class. With the assistance of my class notes, an important reference material, I was able to eliminate previous errors and find the correct solutions. What had once seemed impossible to understand was now starting to make sense. The more it became clear to me, the more intrigued I became with physics. By the time finals arrived I felt prepared and confident that I could conquer whatever was laid before me. I walked out of the exam with a sense of accomplishment and personal satisfaction. My efforts and hard work had paid off. This was confirmed by a phone call I received from Dr. Kalman himself. He was phoning to congratulate me on the remarkable improvement I had made since the midterm. Although I do not foresee a career as a physicist in my near future I have a newfound respect for myself. I came to understand that physics is not a course that requires memorization. It requires hard work and comprehension of the course material. This is an excellent class and a good opportunity for personal growth. I wish all of you the best of luck and just remember, nothing is impossible!

Reprinted with permission.

9

Methods for Training Students to Solve Problems

This chapter presents two methods to help students solve problems the way experts solve problems—they include the use of reflective writing and having students solve problems as members of a collaborative group.

Writing Their Way Into the Solution

Students who have major difficulties in solving quantitative physics problems can be taught to solve complex problems by writing their way into the solution. Many students are afraid to put down something "wrong" on the paper—they don't want to look bad. In particular, students have told me that they find red marks on their work distressing.

Often I get notes written at the end of an exam. One such note said,

> I don't know what happened to me today, but I feel as though I just did not succeed during this exam, I felt okay coming in, and I worked extremely hard this year as I think my marks up to this point reflect. I don't know what to say. I felt overwhelmed and

> confused by this exam and these questions. Obvi-
> ously, I have a lot to learn about problem solving.

After correcting her exam, I asked her why she wrote the note. She said that something strange had happened. When she finished the exam, she couldn't remember anything that she had written and her head really hurt. She had never had that kind of experience before. That had convinced her that she had done poorly on the exam. She actually had written a perfect exam. There was not one error. What she had been doing was practicing reflective writing to write herself into the solution of the problems. In my opinion, this student had never concentrated so hard before in her life and that is why her head hurt. She wrote a letter for students that I always read at the beginning of my course (see Appendix 9.1). I encourage you to read it to your students if you think it will help them.

Another student wrote after her final exam:

> Concerning the final exam: it was the first time that I
> had an idea how to solve the problems without
> searching for hours. I guess that I was just starting
> to understand the concepts. . . . I now think that
> most of the answers are in the concepts and I can
> understand better why you are trying this reflective
> writing.

Lochhead and Whimbey (1987) note that "an even deeper level of understanding is demanded when students are asked to explain their thinking at a level that someone who knew little mathematics could understand" (p. 86). This is the same kind of deep understanding that occurs when students use writing to solve problems. They effectively explain the problem to themselves.

Students who have difficulty in science/engineering courses because they can't seem to solve complex quantitative science/engineering problems can write themselves into the solution by effectively dialoguing about the problem with themselves, thus engaging their whole brain on the problem, not just the conscious part.

Collaborative Problem-Solving Groups

Problem solving is a mainstay of all science/engineering courses. It is usually a large fraction of or the sole component of examinations in the course. As discussed in Chapter 3, students often think that the problems are independent of the concepts and principles taught in the courses. They ask me to stop spending so much time discussing concepts and to spend more time covering assignments. If I have a good TA in a recitation section, students will occasionally write on their course evaluations that "If it weren't for the TA, I couldn't manage the course." Experiments investigating the effects of collaborative group learning on the problem-solving abilities of college students in large introductory courses have been reported by Heller, Keith, and Anderson (1992) and Heller and Hollabaugh (1992). Heller and her coauthors use a collaborative group approach that "combines the explicit teaching of a problem solving strategy with a supportive environment to help students implement the strategy" (Heller et al., 1992, p. 627). Their idea is that "in well-functioning cooperative groups, students share their conceptual and procedural knowledge as they solve a problem together" (p. 635).

Heller and her coauthors also feel that collaborative problem solving puts fewer demands on the instructor. Recitation section leaders can with minimal training implement the procedures. Students can consult each other on explanations and justifications. In the process, students can understand the other group members' views on the concepts and collectively clarify their understanding of the concepts. The various strategies that each member uses for solving problems is revealed and become the mutual property of all group members. I always encourage students to work in groups on problems. In my course outline, I note that up to four students may submit a single solution with the names and ID numbers of all students on the solution.

In Heller's study, students were taught general problem-solving strategies based on the literature describing how experts solve problems (Chi, Glaser, & Rees, 1990; Larkin, McDermott, Simon, & Simon, 1980). Then they constructed practice and test problems that highlighted the strategies. (Some of the sample problems are analyzed in their articles.) Next, during recitation and laboratory sessions, students were placed in carefully managed collaborative groups and worked together under the supervision of the recitation leaders.

To train students to utilize the five-step procedure, students were placed in collaborative groups containing three or four members in the recitation and laboratory sessions. Initially the students were randomly assigned to the groups, but after the first test, students were purposively assigned. Each group consisted of a student from each of the top, middle, and lower sections of the class. Students were assigned the roles of manager, skeptic, and checker/recorder and these roles were rotated each week.

Heller et al. (1992) examined whether *all* students improved in their problem-solving abilities over the period that the students were in the courses. They compared the performances over time of each of the top, middle, and bottom thirds of the class and found that all the groups had improved in their abilities to solve problems. The students were also compared against students in other sections of the course who had been taught in the traditional manner without collaborative problem-solving groups. The students who had received training in collaborative problem solving did significantly better in solving problems than the students enrolled in the traditional sections. The biggest reason for the difference in the results was in the use of qualitative methods for the analysis of the problems. All students in the experimental section used force diagrams to solve a problem, compared to only 57% of those in the traditional sections. One major feature of this approach is a shift in the students' approach to solving problems from "what formula should we use" to "what concepts and principles do we need to employ in solving this problem."

How Many People Should Be in the Group?

Heller and Hollabaugh (1992) experimented with groups of two to four students. They found that in the larger groups, the group was more likely to jump to a newer, more fruitful approach rather than continue to follow a sterile mode of trying to solve the problem. In the case of pairs, the discussion was usually dominated by one partner, "so that the pair normally did not function as a collabora-tive group" (Heller & Hollabaugh, p. 640).

If each of the partners had a strongly held view, there never seemed to be a mechanism for deciding between them, so the pair seemed to follow the lead of the dominant partner, even if the dom-inate partner had the wrong approach. In larger groups, when two members had opposing suggestions for procedures, another group member was likely to step in to mediate between the two partners. If a total impasse was reached, the groups usually resorted to vot-ing, which had a better chance of leading the group to the correct choice, than a choice resulting from domination by one group member. Groups of four had some problems compared to the groups of three. One member inevitably was left out of the group deliberations (Heller & Hollabaugh, 1992).

Sometimes this was the most timid member of the group. At other times this was the most knowledgeable member of the group, who seemed to tire in the face of the constant struggle to convince the other three members to try a particular approach and would then simply solve the problem on his or her own, without any help from the other students. So groups of three seem to be optimal.

In my own use of groups in large-enrollment classes for other purposes than problem solving, I usually have to resort to four or five students to a group. Some students inevitably withdraw from the course, so a group of three can quickly be reduced to one after the midterm.

Who Should Be Placed in the Group?

Heller and Hollabaugh (1992) note that groups containing one high-ability, one medium-ability, and one low-ability student per-formed as well as groups containing only high-ability students, so it is better to mix the students so that the poorer students can learn from the better students. Indeed, groups containing only high-abil-ity students sometimes took longer to solve problems than the mixed-ability students. They tended to go for complex methods, sometimes missing obvious methods, then finding the simpler methods only after wasting a lot of time.

Individual Accountability

Several problems were encountered with Heller's groups. Some students missed all or almost all of the group problem-solving sessions, but would show up for the group test. This was countered by establishing a rule that if a student was absent for a group problem-solving session prior to a test, they would automatically receive a grade of zero on the test.

Recitation leaders routinely quizzed the student who was least involved in the group problem-solving sessions. Also at the subsequent class sessions, instructors randomly called on students to present the solution to the problem.

Summary

- *A kind of deep understanding occurs when students use writing to solve problems. They effectively explain the problem to themselves. Students who have difficulty in science/engineering courses because they can't solve complex quantitative science/engineering problems can write themselves into the solution because they effectively dialogue about the problem with themselves.*

- *Heller and her coauthors use a collaborative group approach. Students can consult each other on explanations and justifications. In the process, students can understand the other group members' views on the concepts and collectively clarify their understanding of them. Heller and her coauthors suggest that collaborative problem solving puts fewer demands on the instructor.*

- *Collaborative groups of three were found to work best for problem solving. Groups that mixed students of varying abilities arrived at solutions faster than groups containing only high-ability students who tended to miss the obvious methods.*

Appendix 9.1

A Student's Advice for Studying Physics

Physics is a very difficult and frustrating science. When I began the Mechanics course, I thought I would never get by. In the first couple of assignments, I spent hours trying to figure out how to do the problems and never seemed to get the right answers. I didn't understand why. During the classes, I followed along and seemed to grasp all of the concepts, and then when I got home, I couldn't do the problems.

What helped me out, unknowing to me, was the concept assignments. When I had to write them up, I didn't enjoy it very much. They seemed long and time consuming, and I felt that I should have spent more time on the problems than the freewriting since I had so much trouble with the problems.

After the midterm, I started to realize that the concepts were extremely important. I did fairly well on the midterm because of two strategies:

1) I did as many problems as I could before the test. I even bought the solutions manual so as to try all the different problems I could. Some I got, some I didn't. The ones I didn't get, I went through step by step from the manual and tried to understand what they were doing. This is where the concepts began to come into play.

2) If there was a problem I couldn't get on the exam, I went through the concepts in order to try and understand what the problem was asking. And for the most part, even if I couldn't get the right answer, I had the concepts and knew at least the gist of the problem.

Another important consideration in studying physics is keeping your cool, and not giving up. If you do as many problems as you can and understand the main concepts, you should be ok. I thought I had failed the final exam. I got so frustrated during the exam; I almost wanted to throw my exam out in the garbage. I couldn't understand why I was so prepared for the exam and felt like I couldn't do anything. That's when the freewriting came into play. I remember one question that I couldn't get at all. But I knew, because of the concepts, what I was being asked and the steps I needed to take in order to find the solution, I just blanked formulating the equation and manipulating the right variables to find the solution. Because I knew the concepts, I didn't lose as many points as I thought I had. (In fact, to my surprise I ended up doing very well on the exam). I didn't give up, I kept going. I think I tried to redo that question three or four times, and finally tried freewriting. Once I free wrote, I figured more out on the problem.

My advice for any prospective students:

1) Do as many problems as possible. Since I did so many problems throughout the semester, I didn't need as much time to study for the final. When you have a full course load, this is very beneficial!

2) Understand the concepts!! This may not seem important to you as you are doing the assignments, but can help you in an exam and even in figuring out homework problems.

3) Stay cool! It's easy to become frustrated while working out problems.

4) Don't be afraid to seek help! The TAs give good tutorials, and Dr. Kalman has office hours for answering questions as well. Physics is very hard, and sometimes all you need is one explanation to understand an entire concept.

Good luck!

Reprinted with permission.

10

Using the Computer to Aid Teaching

Using computers to give tutorial lessons and how to use the computer to manage laboratories are discussed in this chapter. A modification of Noah Sherman's (1971) templates is presented that can easily be used to construct tutorial programs. Also included is a tutorial program that I have used with some success in my classroom. Currently all of the programs found in this book are being written for web-based access.

Computer-Assisted Instruction

After noting successes of using the computer as an aid to instruction, McKeachie (1986) states that "the major reason that Computer-Assisted Instruction (CAI) has not spread more rapidly is the time consuming, difficult work necessary to develop a system that uses the memory and adaptive capacity of the computer" (p. 154). The answer to this conundrum is to develop a computer system that is easy to use. That is, one that a professor can use to easily convert a set of questions into an effective computer tutorial (CAI).

In 1971, I set out to develop such a program as my first incursion into scientific educational research. To understand the implementation of CAI in science courses, I decided to first implement someone else's CAI program on our campus computer system, and then try my hand on my own dialogue. When it came to the dialogue, it was first decided to develop a computer language (Kalman & Kaufman, 1974) that would make it easy for us to write our dialogue and also could be used by others to write their own dialogues. I decided to adapt Noah Sherman's (1971) as the basis for our language. Our adaptation is shown in Figure 10.1.

FIGURE 10.1

Computer-Assisted Instruction Dialogue

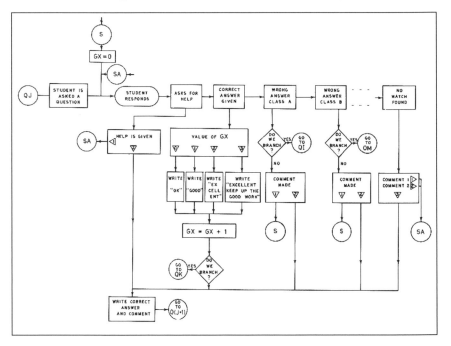

Students respond to questions supplied by the program in natural language. Current implementations could give students the option of *talking* to the computer or typing in a response. The computer scans the responses for keywords, and responses correspond to the class of keywords found by the computer. Our implementation incorporates three modifications of Sherman's original templates. First, a special "help" class has been added; that is, if students use the word *help* or a synonym in their response, they receive immediate assistance. Second, a student with successive correct responses is given more encouraging responses. ("OK" for one correct response, "good" for two correct responses in a row, "excellent" for three in a row, and "excellent, keep up the good work" for four in a row.) Finally and most important, the possibility of branching has been introduced. Thus, depending on the student's response, the student might be directed to any other question instead of proceeding to the next question in the sequence.

In our implementation, we preceded the tutorial with a CAI pretest (see Figure 10.2). The purpose of the pretest is to check that the student has the required background to understand the material presented in the tutorial (see Figure 10.3). No attempt to teach is made in the pretest. Typically, there are only two answer classes in the pretest: one correct class consisting of all acceptable keywords and one wrong class corresponding to any other response. The correct answer permits the student to proceed to the next question. An incorrect response could lead to ejection from the program. Alternatively, a student could proceed through the entire pretest and receive a report of any deficiencies.

FIGURE 10.2

Adaptation of Noah Sherman's Templates for Pretests

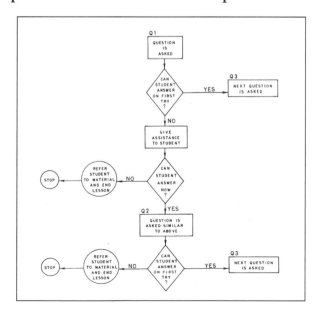

FIGURE **10.3**

Pretest

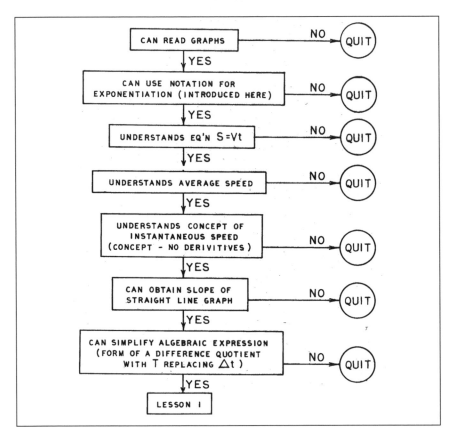

Careful testing of questions is necessary. Our CAI calculus dialogues were introduced during a summer session. We tried the dialogues on a few students at a time, then immediately interviewed the students to learn why they chose the answer they did for each question. Their responses provided us with additional keywords, alterations in the language of the questions, and pointed out the need for logic changes in the programs. Then, before the next few students made their attempt, we would edit the dialogues. We also discovered that the original dialogue was too long and needed to be split into two parts. By the end of the summer session, we had confidence in our dialogues, which are found in Figures 10.4 and 10.5.

FIGURE 10.4

Lesson 1

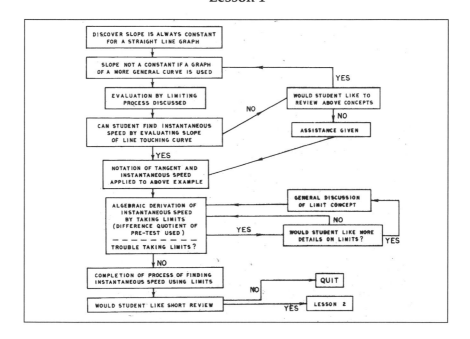

FIGURE 10.5

Lesson 2

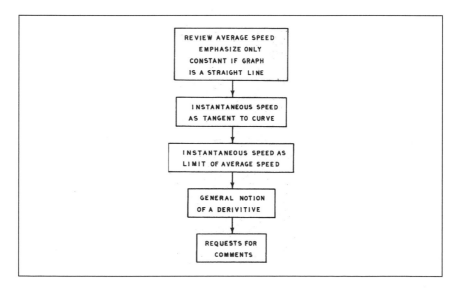

The problem that we were trying to resolve was the use of calculus in the first of the three introductory courses. The calculus course always lags behind the physics course, and students always have difficulties with the brief explanations given by the physics instructors. Comparisons in the fall with students in a control group using the posttest found in Figure 10.6 indicated significant improvement in student understanding with the CAI instruction. For a successful CAI dialogue, it is important to use short presentations of material/questions, many opportunities for interactive activity, careful testing of the questions, and plenty of opportunities for "looping."

Using the Computer to Manage Laboratories

At Concordia University, we began using an automated computer managed laboratory system in 1966. This system has been described in an anonymous article in the *Canadian University* magazine (Covered benches, 1967), Tomas (1971), and Kalman (1987). The key part of the program is to have all the experiments in the laboratories set up permanently and open for a significant amount of time during the academic year.

The idea of operating a science "library of experiments" was first proposed by Oppenheimer and Correll (1964). Students may visit the "library" any time that it is open and, having booked time, perform experiments for their course. Since the labs are open for extended periods of time, far fewer lab setups are required. Aside from cost savings on laboratory equipment, this requirement of fewer lab setups makes it possible to have available all the experiments used during an entire semester within the same space traditionally required for the laboratories.

There is a concomitant savings in technicians. Since the laboratories are permanently set up, one full-time lab supervisor, one full-time technician, and one storekeeper are all that is required to service the entire operation. Storekeepers are students who are employed on part-time contracts.

We ensure that students are familiar with the equipment and the background of each laboratory by having them use computers

FIGURE 10.6

Posttest

1) What is the name for the slope of a straight line segment joining two points on the graph of distance vs, time ?

2) What is the name for the slope of a straight line segment which is tangent to the curve of distance vs. time ?

3) What is the name for the limit of average speed in an interval as the size of that interval approaches zero ?

4) What is the name for the slope of a straight line segment which is tangent to the curve of Y vs. X and is written as DY/DX ?

5)

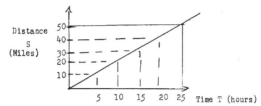

Calculate the average speed in the interval between
t = 5 to t = 20 hours ?

6)

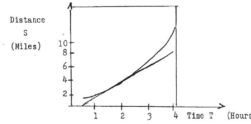

a) Compute the average speed (in hours) in the interval from t = 1 to t = 4 hours, in the graph above.

b) Compute the instantaneous speed at t = 2 from the graph above

7) Evaluate the following limits:

a) $\lim_{\Delta t \to 0} (3t + 4\Delta t - 6)$

b) $\lim_{\Delta t \to 0} \left[4t(\Delta t)^2 + 2(\Delta t) + 5t \right]$

8) Define the instantaneous speed v, at any time t, as a function of distance S and time t.

9) Given that $S = t^2 + 8$ represents the distance S of a boat at any time t.

a) Compute the average speed between t = 1 and t = 1 + t.

b) Compute the instantaneous speed at t = 1.

10) Given an equation $y = x^2 - 2$.

Evaluate the derivative of y with respect to x at x = 4,
which is written as dy/dx. Use the limit definition.

in the lab to take a pretest for every specific experiment. Students may not take any material with them during pretests. Any student attempting an experiment without taking the pretest receives a grade of zero for the experiment.

Since students are familiar with the experiment before entering the lab, very few demonstrators need to be available during the hours of operation. A single demonstrator covers the three introductory laboratories corresponding to the three introductory courses that cover introductory calculus-based physics. One further demonstrator covers the 14 advanced labs. During peak periods at the beginning of the year, one extra demonstrator is needed. Demonstrators are students who are employed on part-time contracts. Typically, the lab hours have been 2:00 p.m.–10:00 p.m. Monday through Thursday, covering an enrollment of 1,000 students in the three introductory labs and 400 in the upper-level laboratories.

After performing each lab, students write tests on lab computers. A single, full-time test room operator monitors the system. For these tests, students are only permitted their data sheets stamped and initialed by a demonstrator. Final lab exams are also administered using the same system. A student presents a university ID card to the test room operator and indicates which test is to be taken (pretest, individual lab test, or final). Immediately after the operator enters the information into the system, a set of randomly selected questions is downloaded to the student's designated computer. During the test, the computer screen always displays the time remaining to perform the test and a calculator program. Within this time, the student can move back and forth between the questions, answering or changing answers as desired. Questions require any of multiple choice, numeric, or essay answers. Numeric questions are based on student results found on their data sheets and are considered correct if the answer falls within an anticipated range. The range is continually revised as the equipment ages. Essay questions are scanned for appropriate keywords.

At the end of the time limit or as soon as students sign off, they receive a grade. In case of dispute, the lab supervisor or the director of labs (a faculty member designated to oversee the laboratories) can have the system recreate the test. When the test is recreated, a special statistics package also provides immediate comparison of the student answers with those given by the previous 20 students who were asked the same question. Due to this package, not a single appeal of grade beyond the director of labs has occurred since the change of the configuration to an entirely computer-managed system.

With this type of system, in addition to cost savings, students learn more, and they are always prepared for the experiments in advance of coming to the lab. Students cannot piggyback on another student, as each student performs every laboratory on their own. Moreover, there is no need to "rotate" students through labs. Students can easily perform all the experiments in a set order.

Summary

- *A professor can easily convert a set of questions into an effective computer tutorial (CAI). Careful testing of questions is necessary. For a successful CAI dialogue, you need to use short presentations of material/questions, many opportunities for interactive activity, careful testing of the questions, and plenty of opportunities for "looping."*

- *Concordia University began using an automated computer managed laboratory system in 1966. The key part of the program is to have all the experiments in the laboratories set up permanently and open for a significant amount of time during the academic year. Since the labs are open for extended periods of time, far fewer lab setups are required. To ensure that students are familiar with the equipment and the background of each laboratory, they take a pretest for every specific experiment on computers in the lab. After performing each lab, students write tests on lab computers. This type of system produces cost savings and students who learn more and are always prepared for experiments before coming to the lab. Students cannot piggyback on another student, as each student performs every laboratory on their own, and there is no need to "rotate" students through labs.*

Suggested Readings

Abrami, P. C., Chambers, B., Poulsen, C., De Simone, C., d'Apollonia, S., & Howden, J. (1995). *Classroom connections: Understanding and using cooperative learning.* Montreal, Canada: Harcourt Brace.

Bork, A. M., & Arons, A. B. (1967, February). Resource letter ColR-1 on collateral reading for physics courses. *American Journal of Physics, 35*(2), 71–78.

Bork, A. M., & Sherman, N. (1971, February). A computer-based dialog for deriving energy conservation for motion in one dimension. *American Journal of Physics, 39*(2), 137–143.

Bowden, J., Dall'Alba, G., Martin, E., Laurillard, D., Marton, F., Masters, G., et al. (1992, March). Displacement, velocity, and frames of reference: Phenomenographic studies of students' understanding and some implications for teaching and assessment. *American Journal of Physics, 60*(3), 262–269.

Chi, M. T. H., Feltovich, P. J., & Glaser, R. (1981). Categorization and representation of physics problems by experts and novices. *Cognitive Science, 5*(2), 121–152.

Correll, M., & Strassenburg, A. A. (1965). Recommendations. In M. Correll & A. A. Strassenburg (Eds.), *The proceedings of the Boulder conference on physics for nonscience majors* (pp. 248–249). New York, NY: Commission on College Physics, American Institute of Physics.

Greenfield, L. (1987). Teaching thinking through problem solving. In J. E. Stice (Ed.), *New directions for teaching and learning: No. 30. Developing critical thinking and problem-solving abilities* (pp. 5–22). San Francisco, CA: Jossey-Bass.

Gunstone, R. F. (1987, August). Student understanding in mechanics: A large population survey. *American Journal of Physics, 55*(8), 691–696.

Heller, J. I., & Reif, F. (1984). Prescribing effective human problem-solving processes: Problem description in physics. *Cognition and Instruction, 1*(2), 177–216.

Holton, G. J., & Brush, S. G. (1985). *Introduction to concepts and theories in physical science* (2nd & rev. ed.). Princeton, NJ: Princeton University Press.

Kalman, J., & Kalman, C. (1996, July). Writing to learn. *American Journal of Physics, 64*(7), 954–955.

Lakatos, I. (1976). *Proofs and refutations: The logic of mathematical discovery.* New York, NY: Cambridge University Press.

Larkin, J. H. (1980). Teaching problem solving in physics: The psychological laboratory and the practical classroom. In D. J. Tuma & F. Reif (Eds.), *Problem solving and education: Issues in teaching and research* (pp. 11–125). Hillsdale, NJ: Lawrence Erlbaum.

Lawson, A. E., & Renner, J. W. (1975, September). Piagetian theory and biology teaching. *The American Biology Teacher, 37*(6), 336–343.

McDermott, L. C., Rosenquist, M. L., & van Zee, E. H. (1987, June). Student difficulties in connecting graphs and physics: Examples from kinematics. *American Journal of Physics, 55*(6), 503–513.

McKinnon, J. W., & Renner, J. W. (1971). Are colleges concerned with intellectual development? *American Journal of Physics, 39*(9), 1047–1052.

Nicolson, M. (1965, March). Resource letter SL–1 on science and literature. *American Journal of Physics, 33*(3), 175–183.

Reif, F., Larkin, J. H., & Brackett, G. C. (1976, March). Teaching general learning and problem solving skills. *American Journal of Physics, 44*(3), 212–217.

Renner, J. W., & Lawson, A. E. (1973, May). Promoting intellectual development through science teaching. *The Physics Teacher, 11*(5), 273–276.

Rosenquist, M. L., & McDermott, L. C. (1987, May). A conceptual approach to teaching kinematics. *American Journal of Physics, 55*(5), 407–415.

Tao, P-K., & Gunstone, R. (1997). The process of conceptual change in force and motion during computer-supported physics instruction. *Journal of Research in Science Teaching, 36*(7), 859–882.

Woods, D. R. (1989). Problem solving in practice. In D. Gabel (Ed.), *What research says to the science teacher: Problem solving* (Vol. 5, pp. 97–121). Washington, DC: National Science Teachers Association.

Bibliography

Anderson, D. L., Fisher, K. M., & Norman, G. J. (2002, December). Development and evaluation of the conceptual inventory of natural selection. *Journal of Research in Science Teaching, 39*(10), 952–978.

Aronson, E., Blaney, N., Stephan, C., Sikes, J., & Snapp, M. (1978). *The jigsaw classroom.* Beverely Hills, CA: Sage.

Barnes, D., Britton, J., & Torbe, M. (1990). *Language, the learner, and the school* (4th ed.). Portsmouth, NH: Boynton/Cook.

Basili, P. A., & Sanford, J. P. (1991). Conceptual change strategies and cooperative group work in chemistry. *Journal of Research in Science Teaching, 28*(4), 293–304.

Belenkey, M. F., Clinchy, B. M., Goldberger, N. R., & Tarule, J. M. (1997). *Women's ways of knowing: The development of self, voice, and mind.* New York, NY: Basic Books.

Bereiter, C., & Scardamalia, M. (1987). *The psychology of written composition.* Hillsdale, NJ: Lawrence Erlbaum.

Berg, R. (1992). *The video encyclopedia of physics demonstrations.* Los Angeles, CA: The Education Group.

Britton, J., Burgess, T., Martin, N., McLeod, A., & Rosen, H. (1975). *The development of writing abilities.* London, England: Macmillan.

Chi, M. T. H., Glaser, R., & Rees, E. (1990). Expertise in problem solving. In R. S. Sternberg (Ed.), *Advances in the psychology of human intelligence* (Vol. 2, pp. 3–30). Hillsdale, NJ: Lawrence Erlbaum.

Chi, M. T. H., Slotta, J. D., & deLeeuw, N. (1994). From things to processes: A theory of conceptual change for learning science concepts. *Learning and Instruction, 4*(1), 27–43.

Cliburn, J. W., Jr. (1990, February). Concept maps to promote meaningful learning. *Journal of College Science Teaching, 19*(4), 212–217.

Coletta, V. P., & Phillips, J. A. (2005, December). Interpreting FCI scores: Normalized gain, preinstruction scores, and scientific reasoning ability. *American Journal of Physics, 73*(12), 1172–1182.

Connolly, P., & Vilardi, T. (Eds.). (1989). *Writing to learn mathematics and science.* New York, NY: Teachers College Press.

Countryman, J. (1992). *Writing to learn mathematics: Strategies that work, K–12.* Portsmouth, NH: Heinemann.

Covered benches raise physics lab efficiency. (1967, January/February). *Canadian University, 42.*

Dedic, H., Rosenfield, S., d'Apollonia, S., & De Simone, C. (1994, Spring). Using cooperative concept mapping in college science classes. *Cooperative Learning and College Teaching, 4*(3), 12–15.

Dewey, J. (1910). *How we think.* Boston, MA: D. C. Heath.

diSessa, A. A. (1993, November). Toward an epistemology of physics. *Cognition and Instruction, 10*(2–3), 105–225.

diSessa, A. A., & Sherin, B. L. (1998). What changes in conceptual change? *International Journal of Science Education, 20*(10), 1155–1191.

Driver, R. (1973). *The representation of conceptual frameworks in young adolescent science students.* Unpublished doctoral dissertation, University of Illinois at Urbana-Champaign.

Duncker, K. (1945). On problem solving. *Psychological Monographs, 58*(5), 1–110.

Duschl, R. A., & Gitomer, D. H. (1991, November). Epistemological perspectives on conceptual change: Implications for educational practice. *Journal of Research in Science Teaching, 28*(9), 839–858.

Elbow, P. (1998). *Writing without teachers*. New York, NY: Oxford University Press.

Elby, A. (2001, July). Helping physics students learn how to learn. *American Journal of Physics, 69*(S1), S54–S64.

Feyerabend, P. (1993). *Against method* (3rd ed.). New York, NY: Verso.

Fulwiler, T. (Ed.). (1987). *The journal book*. Portsmouth, NH: Boynton/Cook.

Gabbert, B., Johnson, D. W., & Johnson, R. T. (1986). Cooperative learning, group-to-individual transfer, process gain, and the acquisition of cognitive reasoning strategies. *Journal of Psychology, 120*(3), 265–278.

Gick, M. L., & Holyoak, K. J. (1980). Analogical problem solving. *Cognitive Psychology, 12*(80), 306–355.

Gick, M. L., & Holyoak, K. J. (1983). Schema induction and analogical transfer. *Cognitive Psychology, 15*(1), 1–38.

Goldschmid, M. I., & Shore, B. M. (1974). The learning cell: A field test of an educational innovation. In W. A. Verrick (Ed.), *Methodological problems in research and development in higher education: Proceedings of the inaugural congress of the European Association for Research and Development in Higher Education* (pp. 218–236). Amsterdam, The Netherlands: Swets & Zeitlinger B.V.

Halloun, I. A., & Hestenes, D. (1985a, November). Common sense concepts about motion. *American Journal of Physics, 53*(11), 1056–1065.

Halloun, I. A., & Hestenes, D. (1985b, November). The initial knowledge state of college physics students. *American Journal of Physics, 53*(11), 1043–1055.

Halpern, D. F. (1997). *Critical thinking across the curriculum: A brief edition of thought and knowledge*. Mahwah, NJ: Lawrence Erlbaum.

Hammer, D. (1989, December). Two approaches to learning physics. *The Physics Teacher, 27*(9), 664–670.

Hammer, D. (1994). Epistemological beliefs in introductory physics. *Cognition and Instruction, 12*(2), 151–183.

Hein, T. L. (1994, December). Using journals to enhance understanding of student misconceptions in an introductory level physics course for non-science majors. *American Association of Physics Teachers Announcer, 24*, 86.

Heinze-Fry, J. A. (1987). Evaluation of concept mapping as a tool for meaningful education of college biology students. *Dissertation Abstracts International, 48*(1), 95A.

Heller, P., & Hollabaugh, M. (1992, July). Teaching problem solving through cooperative grouping. Part 2: Designing problems and structuring groups. *American Journal of Physics, 60*(7), 637–644.

Heller, P., Keith, R., & Anderson, S. (1992, July). Teaching problem solving through cooperative grouping. Part 1: Group versus individual problem solving. *American Journal of Physics, 60*(7), 627–636.

Hestenes, D., Wells, M., & Swackhamer, G. (1992, March). Force concept inventory. *The Physics Teacher, 30*(3), 141–158.

Hewitt, P. G. (1995, September). Lessons from Lily on the introductory course. *Physics Today, 48*, 85–86.

Hewitt, P. G. (2006). *Conceptual physics* (10th ed.). San Francisco, CA: Benjamin Cummings.

Hewson, P., & Hewson, M. (1984). The role of conceptual conflict in conceptual change and the design of scientific instruction. *Instructional Science, 13*(1), 1–13.

Horton, C. (2001, June). *Student preconceptions and misconceptions in chemistry.* Integrated physics and chemistry modeling workshop, Tempe, AZ.

Huffman, D., & Heller, P. (1995, March). What does the force concept inventory really measure? *Physics Teacher, 33*(3), 138–143.

Inhelder, B., & Piaget, J. (1958). *The growth of logical thinking from childhood to adolescence: An essay on the construction of formal operational structures.* New York, NY: Basic Books.

Jensen, V. (1987). Writing in college physics. In T. Fulwiler (Ed.), *The journal book* (pp. 330–336). Portsmouth, NH: Boynton/Cook.

Johnson, D. W., Johnson, R. T., & Smith, K. A. (1991). *Active learning: Cooperation in the college classroom.* Edina, MN: Interaction Book Company.

Kalman, C., & Kaufman, D. (1974, March). Loyola CAI language. *Newsletter of the Associate Committee on Instructional Technology, 3,* 25–30.

Kalman, C. S. (1987, January). A computer-managed undergraduate physics laboratory. *American Journal of Physics, 55*(1), 46–47.

Kalman, C. S. (1998, January/February). Developing critical thinking using cooperative learning techniques. *Physics in Canada,* 15–17.

Kalman, C. S. (1999). Teaching science to non-science students using a student-centred classroom. In S. Fallows & K. Ahmet, *Inspiring students: Case studies in motivating the learner* (pp. 17–24). London, England: Kogan Page.

Kalman, C. S. (2002, January). Developing critical thinking in undergraduate courses: A philosophical approach. *Science and Education, 11*(1), 83–94.

Kalman, C. S., Kaufman, D., & Smith, R. (1974, May). Introductory CAI dialogue in differential calculus for freshman physics. *American Journal of Physics, 42*(5), 392–395.

Kalman, C. S., Morris, S., Cottin, C., & Gordon, R. (1999, July). Promoting conceptual change using collaborative groups in quantitative gateway courses. *American Journal of Physics, 67*(S1), S45–S51.

Kalman, C. S., Rohar, S., & Wells, D. (2004, May). Enhancing conceptual change using argumentative essays. *American Journal of Physics, 72*(5), 715–717.

Kalman, J., & Kalman, C. S. (1997). Writing to learn. *Essays on Teaching Excellence, 9*(4).

Kirkpatrick, L. D., & Pittendrigh, A. S. (1984, March). A writing teacher in the classroom. *The Physics Teacher, 22*(3), 159–164.

Kuhn, T. S. (1970). *The structure of scientific revolutions* (2nd ed.). Chicago, IL: University of Chicago Press.

Kuhn, T. S. (1996). *The structure of scientific revolutions* (3rd ed.). Chicago, IL: University of Chicago Press.

Lakatos, I. (1970). Falsification and the methodology of scientific research programmes. In I. Lakatos & A. Musgrave (Eds.), *Criticism and the growth of knowledge* (pp. 91–196). New York, NY: Cambridge University Press.

Larkin, J. H., McDermott, J., Simon, D. P., & Simon, H. A. (1980, June). Expert and novice performance in solving physics problems. *Science, 208*(20), 1335–1342.

Larkin-Hein, T., & Budny, D. D. (2001, October). *Learning the "write" way in science and engineering.* Paper presented at the 31st annual ASEE/IEEE Frontiers in Education Conference, Reno, NV.

Lochhead, J., & Whimbey, A. (1987). Teaching analytical reasoning through thinking aloud pair problem solving. In J. E. Stice (Ed.), *New directions for teaching and learning: No. 30. Developing critical thinking and problem-solving abilities* (pp. 73–92). San Francisco, CA: Jossey–Bass.

Matthews, M. R. (1994). *Science teaching: The role of history and philosophy of science.* New York, NY: Routledge.

McDermott, L. C. (1984, July). Research on conceptual understanding in mechanics. *Physics Today, 37*(7), 24–32.

McKeachie, W. J. (1986). *Teaching tips: A guidebook for the beginning college teacher* (8th ed.). Lexington, MA: D. C. Heath.

McLaughlin, M. (1995). *Employability skills profile: What are employers looking for?* Retrieved September 13, 2006, from www.ericdigests.org/1997-2/skills.htm

Michener, J. (1975). *Centennial.* New York, NY: Random House.

Mullin, W. (1989a, May). Writing in physics. *The Physics Teacher,* 27(5), 342–347.

Mullin, W. (1989b). Writing in physics. In P. Connolly & T. Vilardi (Eds.), *Writing to learn mathematics and science* (pp. 198–208). New York, NY: Teachers College Press.

Nelson, C. (1994). Critical thinking and collaborative learning. In K. Bosworth & S. J. Hamilton (Eds.), *New directions for teaching and learning: No. 59. Collaborative learning: Underlying processes and effective techniques* (pp. 45–57). San Francisco, CA: Jossey-Bass.

Oppenheimer, F., & Correll, M. (1964, March). A library of experiments. *American Journal of Physics, 32*(3), 220–225.

Pais, A. (1997). *A tale of two continents: A physicist's life in a turbulent world.* Princeton, NJ: Princeton University Press.

Panitz, T. (1995, April 21). *Classroom warm-up exercises for students.* Message posted to Professional and Organizational Development Network in Higher Education electronic mailing list at pod@lists.acs.ohio-state.edu

Piaget, J. (1929). *The child's conception of the world.* New York, NY: Harcourt Brace.

Piaget, J. (1973). *To understand is to invent.* New York, NY: Grossman.

Piaget, J. (1977). The development of thought: Equilibration of cognitive structures (A. Rosin, Trans.). New York, NY: Viking Press. (Original work published 1975)

Pintrich, P., Marx, R. W., & Boyle, R. A. (1993, Summer). Beyond cold conceptual change: The role of motivational beliefs and classroom contextual factors in the process of conceptual change. *Review of Educational Research, 63*(2), 167–199.

Popper, K. R. (1963). *Conjectures and refutations: The growth of scientific knowledge.* New York, NY: Routledge & Kegan Paul.

Posner, G., Strike, K., Hewson, P., & Gertzog, W. (1982). Accommodation of a scientific conception: Toward a theory of conceptual change. *Science Education, 66,* 211–227.

Posner, H. B., & Markstein, J. A. (1994, February). Cooperative learning in introductory cell and molecular biology. *Journal of College Science Teaching, 23*(4), 231–233.

Prigo, R. B. (1978, July). Piagetian-styled and process-based physics lecture course for liberal arts majors. *American Journal of Physics, 46*(7), 752–757.

Pugalee, D. K. (1997, April). Connecting writing to the mathematics curriculum. *The Mathematics Teacher, 90*(4), 308–310.

Redish, E. F. (2003). *Teaching physics.* New York, NY: Wiley.

Renner, J. W., & Lawson, A. E. (1973, March). Piagetian theory and instruction in physics. *The Physics Teacher, 11*(3), 165–169.

Renner, J. W., & Paske, W. C. (1977, September). Comparing two forms of instruction in college physics. *American Journal of Physics, 45*(9), 851–860.

Rivard, L. P. (1994). A review of writing-to-learn in science: Implications for practice and research. *Journal of Research on Science Teaching, 31*(9), 969–983.

Roth, M-W., & Lucas, K. B. (1997, February). From "truth" to "invented reality": A discourse analysis of high school physics students' talk about scientific knowledge. *Journal of Research in Science Teaching, 34*(2), 145–179.

Roy, H. (1996). *Teaching studio genetics and evolution.* Troy, NY: Rensselaer Polytechnic Institute, Department of Biology.

Roy, H. (1999). *Automated testing and measurement of student progress in genetics and evolution.* Retrieved September 19, 2006, from the Rensselaer Polytechnic Institute, Department of Biology web site: www.rpi.edu/~royh/AutomatedTestingAndMeasurement.html

Rubinstein, M. F., & Firstenberg, I. R. (1987). Tools for thinking. In J. E. Stice (Ed.), *New directions for teaching and learning: No. 30. Developing critical thinking and problem-solving abilities* (pp. 23–36). San Francisco, CA: Jossey-Bass.

Salomon, G., & Perkins, D. N. (1989). Rocky roads to transfer: Rethinking mechanisms of a neglected phenomena. *Educational Psychologist, 24*(2), 113–142.

Schermerhorn, S. M., Goldschmid, M. I., & Shore, B. M. (1975, August). Learning basic principles of probability in student dyads: A cross-age comparison. *Journal of Educational Psychology, 67*(4), 551–557.

Schmidt, H-J. (1997). Students' misconceptions—Looking for a pattern. *Science Education, 81*(2), 123–135.

Sherman, N. (1971). Templates for computer assisted instruction. In *Computers in undergraduate science education: Proceedings of a conference on the use of computers in undergraduate science education, August 1970* (pp. 355–361). New York, NY: Commission on College Physics, American Institute of Physics.

Sternberg, R. J. (1990, January). Thinking styles: Keys to understanding student performance. *Phi Delta Kappan, 71*(5), 366–371.

Strike, K. A., & Posner, G. J. (1985). A conceptual change view of learning and understanding. In L. H. T. West & A. L. Pines (Eds.), *Cognitive structures and conceptual change* (pp. 211–231). Orlando, FL: Academic Press.

Strike, K. A., & Posner, G. J. (1992). A revisionist theory of conceptual change. In R. A. Duschl & R. J. Hamilton (Eds.), *Philosophy of science, cognitive psychology, and educational theory and practice* (pp. 147–176). Albany, NY: State University of New York Press.

Tomas, F. (1971, October). Automation in physics laboratories. *The Physics Teacher, 9*(7), 390–391.

Toulmin, S. (1972). *Foresight and understanding: An inquiry into the aims of science.* Princeton, NJ: Princeton University Press.

Treisman, P. (1986). A study of the mathematics performance of black students at the University of California, Berkeley. *Dissertation Abstracts International, 47,* 1641A.

Tuckman, B., & Jensen, M. A. C. (1977). Stages of small group development revisited. *Group and Organization Studies, 2*(4), 419–427.

VanderStoep, S. W., & Seifert, S. M. (1994). Problem solving, transfer, and thinking. In D. T. Tuma & F. Reif (Eds.), *Problem solving and education: Issues in teaching and research* (pp. 27–49). Hillsdale, NJ: Lawrence Erlbaum.

Van Dijk, T., & Kintsch, W. (1983). *Strategies of discourse comprehension.* New York, NY: Academic Press.

Vosniadou, S., & Brewer, W. F. (1987). Theories of knowledge restructuring in development. *Review of Educational Research, 57*(1), 51–67.

Vygotsky, L. S. (1978). *Mind in society: The development of higher psychological processes.* Cambridge, MA: Harvard University Press.

Wallace, J. D., & Mintzes, J. J. (1990, December). The concept map as a research tool: Exploring conceptual change in biology. *Journal of Research in Science Teaching, 27*(10), 1033–1052.

West, E. (1997). *201 icebreakers: Group mixers, warm-ups, energizers, and playful activities.* New York, NY: McGraw-Hill.

Wright, A. (1995, May 18). *Re: Classroom Warmups.* Message posted to the Society for Teaching and Learning in Higher Education electronic mailing list at STLHE-L@unb.ca

Index